D0424827

CHARLOTTE MOTOR SPEEDWAY

HISTORY

WITHDRAWN FROM
COLLECTION

CHARLOTTE MOTOR SPEEDWAY

HISTORY

FROM GRANITE TO GOLD

DEB WILLIAMS

Charleston   London

THE
History
PRESS

Published by The History Press
Charleston, SC 29403
www.historypress.net

Copyright © 2013 by Deb Williams
All rights reserved

Back cover, top: Charlotte Motor Speedway. *Courtesy of John Davison.*

First published 2013

Manufactured in the United States

ISBN 978.1.62619.018.4

Library of Congress CIP data applied for.

Notice: The information in this book is true and complete to the best of our knowledge. It is offered without guarantee on the part of the author or The History Press. The author and The History Press disclaim all liability in connection with the use of this book.

All rights reserved. No part of this book may be reproduced or transmitted in any form whatsoever without prior written permission from the publisher except in the case of brief quotations embodied in critical articles and reviews.

Dedicated to those who have played a role in making Charlotte Motor Speedway the first-class facility it is today, and to my parents, Ray and Cricket Williams, who have always supported me and cultivated my love of stock car racing.

CONTENTS

FOREWORD

I once said Charlotte is the heart and soul of this sport; they just keep all the money in Daytona. And I still feel that way.

From the first time I set my eyes on Charlotte Motor Speedway in 1972 until this day, it has held a special place in my heart. If you win at Charlotte Motor Speedway, it puts you in an elite group of drivers. It says something about your ability to drive; it says something about who you are.

When I began competing in what was then known as the Winston Cup Series, I only drove in five races that first season so that I wouldn't lose my eligibility to compete for rookie honors. The October Charlotte race was my final race that year. I was very blessed when I went there that I fell into a group of people who had been in this sport for a long time. One of those people was my crew chief, Jake Elder. He was one of the all-time great crew chiefs along with Herb Nab, Harry Hyde, Leonard Wood and a few others.

Because of Jake, I had a sense of history, a sense of importance, when it came to Charlotte Motor Speedway. At that time, they had what they called the Triple Crown—the Daytona 500, the Southern 500 and the World 600. That made Charlotte Motor Speedway part of the Triple Crown with its World 600 event. It also was the home track for everyone competing in the sport, and Jake made sure I knew that. You sensed that it was the home track as soon as you arrived at the speedway, even though it wasn't the showplace then that it is now. When you drove into the infield, there were large old volcanic rocks and a big hole. You sat on the dirt bank beside the garage area at a little sign-in building waiting to get your money after the race, talking to Walter Ballard, Richard Childress, Frank Warren, Ed Negre and Raymond Williams.

I happened to run really well in my first Charlotte race, finishing sixth and winning a Rookie of the Race award. From that point on, Charlotte Motor Speedway produced a lot of memories for me.

MORTON MANDAN PUBLIC LIBRARY

In 1980, I was going for three straight wins in the race they now call the Coca-Cola 600. That 600 was probably the longest one we've ever run due to the rain delay. It was almost dark when it finally ended, and it had started a little after noon. It came down to Benny Parsons and me at the end, and it was a real battle between us. In fact, we swapped the lead eight times in the final twenty-six laps. I lost that race by half a car length at the checkered flag.

I was fortunate to win that six-hundred-mile race five times and the five-hundred-mile race once, as well as the inaugural Winston All-Star race. I also got to enjoy being a winning car owner at Charlotte Motor Speedway. Terry Labonte drove my Busch Series (now Nationwide) car to victory in the only four-hundred-mile race held for that division at that track.

There's no doubt Charlotte Motor Speedway is special. From the first All-Star race to the last 600 we've had there, everybody always puts something special together for Charlotte. Dale Earnhardt, Robert Gee and I would always try to one-up each other when we'd prepare our cars for that Saturday (Nationwide) race. We'd always see who could put the most chrome on their car and whose car was the nicest and fastest. That place always brought out the most competition among all of us, more than any other track I can think of.

When you hear the words Charlotte Motor Speedway there are two people you think of: Humpy Wheeler and Bruton Smith. Now some people may remember Richard Howard. I do. He's the guy who brought Chevrolet back to racing in the '70s when Junior Johnson showed up with Charlie Glotzbach. That just shows you that people have always tried to show up at Charlotte with something special. Think about the All-Star races. That's the first time you saw people with unique paint schemes. Dale Earnhardt had one. I had my chrome car. They lit the racetrack, which people thought was bizarre. Now they have the big TV back there.

When I think about Richard Howard, Bruton Smith, Humpy Wheeler and now Marcus Smith, I think about the incredible things they have done with that racetrack. Think about those pre-race shows. They're incredible! They do things in those shows that are similar to ones at a circus. That's the one thing that place has always been known for: putting on a show.

From the first time I went there in '72 until the last time I was there, that place has never disappointed me in the show they put on, the race they put on or the atmosphere they create. Charlotte Motor Speedway is unique, and it always sets an example for all the other racetracks. And, like I said before, it holds a special place in my heart.

Darrell Waltrip

ACKNOWLEDGEMENTS

In October 1967, Charlotte Motor Speedway wasn't anywhere close to being the exquisite facility that exists today, but I knew the minute I saw it and felt its soil beneath my tennis shoes that it was something special. The large shade trees were beautiful and, in direct contrast to a racetrack, brought serenity. The old two-story yellow farmhouse where my dad bought our race tickets intrigued me. That day, at age thirteen, I fell in love with Charlotte Motor Speedway. It was then I knew that one day I wanted to live in the Charlotte, North Carolina area and work in stock car racing. A first cousin and his family had moved to Charlotte a few years earlier from our hometown in the North Carolina mountains, and I always hung on every word as he described the city that, to me, was stock car racing's capital.

Every year on Memorial Day weekend, my attention always turned to Charlotte Motor Speedway and Indianapolis, but my desire was to be in Charlotte. A neighbor even presented me with tickets to the 1972 World 600 as a high school graduation gift, and it was that day, as I started through the gate and looked up at the press box, that I promised myself in ten years I would be there, covering an event. I made it in seven. Therefore, when the opportunity to write Charlotte Motor Speedway's history presented itself to me, I was ecstatic.

However, this labor of love wouldn't have been possible without the assistance and support of many people at Charlotte Motor Speedway. The unlimited access to the speedway's archives was critical to this book's success, so to speedway president Marcus Smith and vice-president of special projects Jessica Fickenscher, I offer a tremendous thank-you. Communications manager Jonathan Coleman was a joy to work with, always assisting me with every request I had and making sure security knew when I would be working in the building. I appreciate security checking with me periodically to make sure I was all right. A special thank-you also goes to Roberta Hood in the communications department, who offered suggestions on where to locate various items.

No book would be complete without interviewing the people who witnessed and experienced much of the subject's history. To those people I am deeply grateful. Thank you, Rick Howard, Bob Moore, Bob Myers, Hill Overton, Pal Parker, Doug Rice, Darrell Waltrip and Humpy Wheeler, for taking time from your busy schedules to talk with me and help me turn this book into a reality. Also, to John Davison and Pal Parker, thank you for going the extra mile to get me several photos that I needed.

A book cannot be produced by one person—it takes a team. The Charlotte Motor Speedway team welcomed me into their family in the early 1980s when I began covering NASCAR races for United Press International, and it's that open door that has allowed me to experience much of the track's history as it occurred. It has been wonderful watching the speedway transform from the track I saw at age thirteen into the multi-racing complex of today. In the early 1990s, I would run the track's frontstretch grandstands with a friend for exercise. Now, I sit at my house when I'm not covering a race, listening to stock cars roar around the track, and smile.

To all my friends who have worked at Charlotte Motor Speedway or remain there today, this book is my thank-you for the instrumental role you have played in helping the facility become the track that every fan wants to visit.

CHAPTER ONE

CHISELING THE GRANITE

During the 1950s, there was no shortage of dirt tracks in the Carolinas or people who wanted to create them. The dusty little bullrings could be found at state fairgrounds or sharing a stadium with a minor-league baseball team. It wasn't uncommon for entrepreneurial men, who were never short on money-making ideas, to take a bulldozer and move dirt around in a field to form a crude, small track, where cars—or jalopies, as they were often called—could rumble around and beat and bang on each other to the delight of the crowd. Clapboard fences would quickly be erected and a turnstile for ticket takers installed. Some of these quickly built community tracks lasted only a season, while others survived for several years. The nation was still rebuilding from its involvement in World War II and the Korean War, and the Southeast's blue-collar worker couldn't get enough of the region's new "bad boys."

Many of the drivers didn't possess the morals and manners that would endear them to the pillars of the community. They were risk takers, many of whom learned their craft by running moonshine. They brought excitement to the South's mill towns and rural areas where life could become rather monotonous and mundane. The automobile industry was exciting, as was developing a car's performance and one's driving skills. High school students and factory workers flocked to the dirt tracks, returned home with their clothes and faces covered in red clay, argued throughout the week about the previous race and then came back for more the next weekend.

Some of the tracks aligned themselves with a sanctioning body, like NASCAR, while others elected to remain independent, happy to cater to the weekly racers. Occasionally, an outsider would be recruited to help unseat the local hero or a bounty placed on a driver if he was winning too much, but there certainly was no shortage of excitement. Fights were commonplace in the pits and not out of the ordinary in the grandstands. The aroma of beer, popcorn and hot dogs often filtered through the dust as the sound of screeching tires and wall-slamming sheet metal caused collective gasps from the crowd seated on wooden bleachers.

Stock car racing was finding its way through the rural South, but there were those who envisioned it growing beyond the dusty bullrings it called home. Two of those men were Curtis Turner and Bruton Smith—a Virginian and North Carolinian, respectively. They were quite different yet similar in that they were independent, flamboyant risk takers and self-made men who had grown up in a rural South that guaranteed only hard work to its residents.

Curtis Morton Turner was born on April 12, 1924, in Floyd, Virginia, a small Shenandoah Mountain town. One of four children, he grew up fast, as was the custom during the Great Depression. He began driving before he was of legal age, hauling his first load of moonshine at age nine. His talent on the narrow, dirt mountain roads became legendary as he honed the driving skills that allowed him to elude the revenuers and local authorities on many occasions. His ability to execute a 180-degree turn—better known as a bootleg or whiskey turn—in a very small space was critical to his success.

Former sportswriter and Rockingham speedway public relations director Herman Hickman recounted in his article on Curtis Turner in the April 1992 edition of *American Racing Classics* how the man with Hollywood good looks enjoyed telling about one federal agent who attempted to catch him hauling liquor thirty-nine times. That agent never succeeded, but Turner was eventually apprehended by a federal agent posted near his father's home. Turner contended it wasn't a fair arrest since the "rule" was if they didn't catch you on the road, you were safe. Still, he paid the $1,000 fine and was given a two-year suspended sentence.

When questioned about those early days, Turner's response was, "Those were hard times back in the hills, and you did things you shouldn't in order to get by. I'm not proud of my past, but I am proud of the future I made for myself. I've made a few fortunes, but I like to live good."

The ruggedly handsome Turner dealt in timber, and he did indeed make and lose more than one fortune during his lifetime. In fact, for Turner, life was a party, and he enjoyed playing the role of a rich man. He maintained you didn't have to be a millionaire as long as you could live like one. Turner made good money and enjoyed spending it on new airplanes and parties. His exploits in airplanes were as wild as his driving.

Curtis Turner envisioned a one-and-a-half-mile racetrack at Charlotte Motor Speedway's current location. *Charlotte Motor Speedway (CMS) Archives.*

One of those adventures landed him in trouble with the Federal Aviation Administration.

It was a typically quiet Sunday morning in Easley, South Carolina, when Turner and an old friend from the town decided, while flying over the friend's home, they would like to have a drink. Turner landed the plane on a street in front of his friend's house so they could get a bottle. However, when Turner got ready to take off again, church services had ended and traffic was coming from several different directions. After hopping over several motorists, Turner finally pulled up at a crossing, taking a stoplight and several dangling wires with him. Telephone service in Easley was cut off, and when he landed in Charlotte, North Carolina, an FAA representative was waiting. The incident grounded Turner for quite some time.

No doubt, stock car racing's wild, rough-and-tumble early days were made for Turner. The six-foot-two Turner threw all-night parties that were famous in the 1950s and early 1960s. In fact, it wasn't unusual for Turner to head directly to the racetrack from a party, hop in his car and compete in an event. It also wasn't unusual to see him napping on his race car's trunk prior to driving the vehicle.

Turner's racing career is listed as officially starting in 1946 following his discharge from the United States Navy. An obscure track in Mount Airy, North Carolina, was where Turner made his racing debut, but he knew nothing about preparing a race car, so the vehicle failed to make it past the halfway mark. The crowd, however, loved his charge-to-the-front, fearless, close-quarter driving style, and Turner knew he wanted more.

Turner dedicated the week after his first race to working on his car, often securing advice. When he showed up at Marion, Virginia, for his second race, he won the event easily and was on his way to quickly building a reputation as one of the best-ever dirt track drivers. In the mid-1950s, *Sports Illustrated* even featured Turner in a story that declared his "350 feature wins made him the Babe Ruth of stock car racing." No one, of course, really knows how many wins Turner secured prior to his NASCAR days because before the sport was officially organized, no one kept records.

It was, however, the creation of NASCAR's convertible division and a contract with Ford that truly put Curtis Turner in the spotlight. He won twenty-two of forty-three convertible races in 1956 and eleven of thirty-one the following year, his only other full season in the ragtops. Overall, he totaled thirty-eight victories in eighty-five starts on the circuit that folded after the 1959 season. In the NASCAR series today known as the Sprint Cup, Turner racked up seventeen victories and the same number of poles in seventeen seasons.

During those hard racing years, Turner and friend Joe Weatherly would bang fenders in an event's later stages. The two Ford drivers called the tactic "popping," and Turner's nickname "Pops" was born.

Throughout his racing and partying, Turner never forgot his lumberman's roots. He had begun lumbering at age fourteen, earning fifteen cents an hour using a crosscut saw. Mountain lore says that by the time he was twenty he had expanded to three sawmills, plus logging equipment and a truck line necessary to keep them going. The influential businessmen Turner met via racing soon discovered the Virginian possessed an uncanny knack for sizing

Bruton Smith shares some ice cream with Miss World 600 Rita Souther of Campobello, South Carolina, prior to the inaugural race. *CMS Archives.*

up a timber patch and estimating the number of board feet it contained by simply flying over the area. When Turner and his associates closed a deal involving about $1 million, a publicist dubbed the country boy a millionaire race car driver. Privately, Turner thought the "millionaire" tag was a joke, but he never attempted to dispel the rumors of his wealth. His parties became "musts" for an increasing number of well-to-do new race fans.

Turner was invited to become a board member of the first Atlanta Speedway organization during its formation. He accepted the offer, and it was then he began thinking about constructing a speedway in Charlotte, where he kept a house on East Boulevard.

Curtis Turner was about a month shy of his third birthday when Ollen Bruton Smith was born on March 3, 1927, in Stanly County, North Carolina, near the small town of Oakboro. Growing up on a cotton farm provided Smith with a strong work ethic during his boyhood years. His family always had plenty of food, but they never had money. That fact played a key role in Smith's desire to become a successful businessman, a desire that was born in Smith's school cafeteria, where Eskimo Pies were sold for a dime. Smith loved ice cream, but he didn't have the ten cents needed to purchase that wonderful product.

"I would see some other students that had that dime, and I remember one of them specifically," Smith said in a 1997 interview. "He was about two grades ahead of me in school. Every day I would see him eating an Eskimo Pie. I thought, 'Gee whiz. His family must have a lot of money.' And I thought, 'Maybe that's where we're short. We're short on money.' I just wanted to one day reach that goal in life where if I wanted an Eskimo Pie I could buy one."

Smith acquired a love for stock car racing at about age seven, when he witnessed his first event and, like most youngsters of that era, decided that he wanted a race car. He finally acquired one at age seventeen, but his mother's opposition ended that potential career before it even had time to get started. After graduating high school, Smith worked briefly in a hosiery mill, but his love for automobiles and racing never diminished. While Turner built a reputation with his daredevil exploits on the track, Smith gravitated to the promoter side of the business. Soon he was working as a car salesman and promoting dirt-track races at the Charlotte Fairgrounds.

In 1949, Bruton Smith headed the National Stock Car Racing Association (NSCRA), one of several fledgling stock car–racing sanctioning bodies and a direct competitor to the National Association for Stock Car Auto Racing, better known as NASCAR. Smith's group sanctioned races in North Carolina, Georgia and Tennessee. When he announced plans in 1949 to establish a "Strictly Stock" division that year, many believed NASCAR head Bill France Sr. accelerated his plans for the same type of series. France's announcement of a 150-mile Strictly Stock race in Charlotte on June 19, 1949, with a $5,000 purse caught nearly everyone off guard. That event was the beginning of today's Sprint Cup Series, but it also triggered a rivalry between the Smith and France families that continued for decades.

A year later, Smith was running Lake Wood Speedway on Highway 16 near Charlotte, but it wasn't a NASCAR-sanctioned track. It was an era when Bill France Sr. didn't like his drivers competing in events not sanctioned by

NASCAR. In an effort to keep the drivers from straying, France instituted a penalty for anyone competing in such an event. The penalty was the removal of championship points. Several drivers received this penalty during their careers, and it cost at least one of them a championship. That driver was Tim Flock. The youngest of ten children, Flock once described the incident that occurred in 1950 as the "worst thing that ever happened in my whole career."

Flock said that after the Modified season ended and he had been declared the series champion, Bruton Smith begged him to run a race for him at his Charlotte track. Flock told Smith he couldn't compete in the race because he was the NASCAR Modified champion and all of his points would be taken from him. France confirmed Flock's statement to Smith when Smith inquired about Flock running his race. Smith then offered Flock $500 to participate in the event. After the monetary offer, the father of five telephoned France and told him he thought he could help Smith attract fans to the event. France reiterated that Flock couldn't compete in the race. Flock ignored France, ran the race and lost his Modified title. After that incident, Flock and France experienced a rocky relationship for the remainder of their lives despite the congenial driver being one of the sport's most popular competitors.

Also in 1950, Smith and France discussed merging their stock car–racing sanctioning organizations and actually reached a tentative agreement. However, before it could be resolved, Smith was drafted into the United States Army in January 1951 to serve as a paratrooper in the Korean War. Upon Smith's return to civilian life, he discovered that mismanagement of the NSCRA during his absence had resulted in the organization being dissolved.

Smith returned to promoting short-track races, and by the time Daytona International Speedway opened in February 1959, he had become an established, well-known short-track promoter. Meanwhile, Curtis Turner had become one of NASCAR's superstars. Turner and NASCAR president Bill France Sr. had even been partners in the 2,176-mile Mexican Road Race in 1950.

With the opening of Daytona, both Turner and Smith envisioned a new direction for stock car racing: the superspeedway. Large, high-banked racetracks made of wooden boards had been popular in the early 1900s, but a high-banked asphalt track where speeds would exceed one hundred miles per hour was an entirely new concept for stock cars. Originally paved with bricks, Indianapolis Motor Speedway was changed to asphalt when it was resurrected after World War II, but it lacked the high banks of the earlier wood tracks. Darlington Raceway in South Carolina, which opened in

1950, was the only banked superspeedway built for stock cars until Raleigh Speedway, a 1-mile paved oval, joined NASCAR in 1953, but it closed shortly thereafter, in 1958. The egg-shaped, 1.366-mile Darlington track with turns that were banked twenty-five and twenty-three degrees remained, but Bill France Sr. possessed a greater vision. With the 1959 opening of France's asphalt, 2.5-mile Daytona track with its thirty-one-degree banked turns, eighteen-degree banked tri-oval and three-degree banked straightaways, Turner and Smith believed a new era for their favorite sport was on the horizon.

On April 22, 1959, Curtis Turner and Bruton Smith held separate news conferences announcing plans to build superspeedways in the Charlotte area. Turner's plans called for a one-and-a-half-mile track named Charlotte Motor Speedway to be built on Highway NC 49. It would have forty-five thousand seats, a one-mile road course and cost $750,000. Smith's announcement called for a two-mile track in Pineville, North Carolina, to be named Charlotte International Speedway. It, too, would have a road course but would have seating for seventy-five thousand and a football field between the frontstretch and pit road. The cost of Smith's plan: $2 million. There was only one major problem: neither man possessed the money needed for their respective projects.

The site Bruton Smith selected after about two months of searching was familiar to race fans. From 1924 to 1926, a superspeedway board track named Charlotte Speedway had operated in the Pineville area, ten miles south of Charlotte's Independence Square. It bordered what's now known as Old Pineville Road, and it was a work of art. Its two turns were banked forty degrees, and the straightaways were eight hundred feet long with the racing surface composed of green pine two-by-fours laid edgewise. It had been constructed by three hundred workers, mostly carpenters, who labored forty days and nights to complete the facility for its opening in 1924. By the time it was finished, four million feet of Carolina lumber and eighty tons of nails and spikes had been used to construct it. The overall cost was placed at nearly half a million dollars.

Jack Prince was the construction engineer, and he did his job so well that the track set the stage for the modernization of other board tracks as well as the standard for those yet to be built. Peter DePaolo piloted a machine bearing the name "Duesenberg" to a 132.8-mile-per-hour lap on the board track in 1925, the same year he won the Indianapolis 500.

The Great Depression was the beautiful board track's demise, but DePaolo perhaps foretold of the sport's future in the Tar Heel State when he wrote: "Everywhere we raced we met people with great interest in our sport, but never in the entire circuit, did we enjoy our visit to a track more than we did the ones we made to North Carolina. The warmth of our greeting was sincere, and it became a custom following each race for us to give the public a statement of thanks and a promise to return."

While Bruton Smith planned his speedway south of Charlotte, Curtis Turner proceeded to work on the one he envisioned north of the Queen City. By May 7, 1959, Turner and his partners—Darlington Raceway builder Harold Brasington, Bowman Gray Stadium promoter Alex Hawkins and North Wilkesboro Speedway promoter Enoch Staley—had formed a corporation to build Charlotte Motor Speedway. Turner was elected president, and the corporation was authorized to issue one million shares of stock at one dollar a share. However, no deal was ever finalized with Turner's proposed site, and a new one had to be selected. The new site consisted of 550 acres just inside Cabarrus County, twelve miles north of Charlotte, on U.S. Highway 29.

The property was hilly and covered with rocks and boulders. In fact, there wasn't a level place on it, but it was cheap at $300 an acre. Decades earlier it had actually been part of neighboring Mecklenburg County. At that time it was the home of Nathaniel Alexander, North Carolina's first elected governor. The house, built in 1774, still stood when the speedway eventually opened. Two cemeteries also remained on small knolls not far from the house when the property was obtained. One, enclosed by a field's ragged stone wall and dotted with marble slabs, was the family's burial ground. The other was the slaves' resting place.

Now, however, more than a century had passed and the placid fields that once hosted George Washington were to receive a different type of hero and host a less genteel visitor.

By June 1959, Smith and Turner had decided to join forces, simply because it was the prudent thing to do financially. Initially, Smith had a verbal agreement with the owner of Propst Construction Company to build a speedway, but he withdrew from the project after suffering a heart attack. Now, Smith and Turner turned to each other. Decades later, Smith admitted he "used" Turner to get what he needed to construct the speedway.

"He was a great name in racing and I needed his name," Smith said in 1997. "I went to him and made a deal with him to use his name and that's all it was. It wasn't a partnership at all, because Curtis did not have very much stock in the speedway."

Smith said Turner attended the groundbreaking festivities for the track but didn't return until it was about 70 percent completed.

Workers install a guardrail around the high-banked turns. *CMS Archives.*

"They hated each other, but they finally decided that to get anything done they had to work together," said Bob Moore, former motorsports writer for the *Charlotte Observer.*

Ground was finally broken for Charlotte Motor Speedway in Cabarrus County, North Carolina, on July 29, 1959. John B. Lippard, a Belmont, North Carolina native and a North Carolina State College School of Design graduate, calculated the mass amount of details that went into constructing Charlotte Motor Speedway. Eighteen-hour days for Lippard at his Landscape Architect and Site Planning office on Elizabeth Avenue in Charlotte were nothing unusual for the soft-spoken man. The forty-one-year-old Lippard said the speedway contained practically every known construction angle and elevation at one place or another. He also noted the five-hundred-foot spirals leading into and out of the twenty-four-degree banked turns demanded endless hours of calculating, not to mention the unique frontstretch and the arrangement of seats on it. Good sight lines for the fans contributed to the track's frontstretch design, but there were other factors as well that were taken into consideration by Smith. The farm boy visionary wanted the track to be more than a speedway.

"Part of that design was a football field (the frontstretch's grassy apron)," Smith explained in an interview published in the March 20, 1997 issue of *NASCAR Winston Cup Scene*. He continued:

> *Before I completed it, I had negotiated a contract with the owner of the Washington Redskins to bring the 'Skins and the Philadelphia Eagles there to play a game. The negotiations were done in the offices of George Marshal, who owned the Washington Redskins at that time. We got so far as the contract was signed by the Philadelphia Eagles. Mr. Marshal hadn't signed yet because he was awaiting a check from me for $40,000. I didn't have the money, but had I been able to give him that $40,000 at that time we would have had football there.*

On September 22, 1959, Turner and Smith flew to Daytona Beach, Florida, to meet with NASCAR president Bill France Sr. and sign the sanctioning agreement for the World 600, Charlotte Motor Speedway's inaugural race and the first six-hundred-mile race for stock cars. It was scheduled for May 29, 1960, and the announced purse was $100,000, the first NASCAR race with posted awards boasting six figures.

However, by the time 1960 arrived, the two men's dream had turned into a nightmare, as the projected costs of about $1 million had proven to be greatly underestimated. Turner, the speedway's first president, said he had the financing all worked out until the contractors hit rock. Turner noted the core-drill report had said it was boulders on the property. So the contract Turner negotiated covered moving dirt and the boulders for eighteen cents a yard. However, it wasn't boulders the constructors hit when they started moving dirt; it was a half-million yards of solid granite. That cost a dollar a yard to move, plus the dynamite that was needed for the job. It took $70,000 worth of dynamite just to get through the first turn. That meant the entire project cost a half million dollars more than it should have, Turner said.

It was a miracle the track was completed, but Turner and Smith, who had been named general manager, made it happen, soliciting money from lenders and always managing to come up with enough funds to continue.

Installing the catch fence along the frontstretch grandstand was a tedious task. *CMS Archives*.

Lights were erected in January so the workers could be divided into two twelve-hour daily shifts in an effort to catch up on the lagging construction that had been hampered by more than ten inches of rain in the last few months of 1959. On January 30–31, fans were invited to the site for an open house in an effort to jump-start ticket sales.

Construction woes worsened in March 1960, when an eleven-inch snow halted all work on the project. Two more snowstorms in the next two weeks followed. Inclement weather, however, wasn't the only problem Smith and Turner faced. Before the first race was held, the two men had accrued $500,000 in outstanding debts.

Initially, Smith was relying on a wealthy brother-in-law who lived in Atlanta for financial support. However, when he was about 60 percent into the project, his brother-in-law suffered a stroke and died. At that time, financial institutions didn't want anything to do with a speedway.

"I'd go to a bank and try to get a capital loan, and they wanted a five-year operating statement," Smith told the media during a 2009 press conference. "I could not get a capital loan. One night I had the idea for a participatory mortgage. I was selling in 5,000 increments where you could invest $5,000 and participate on a $600,000 mortgage. I started raising money and I raised $465,000."

However, the contractor wasn't satisfied. He filed a lien, which granted him a legal claim or hold on the property until he was paid.

Large holes that appeared in the newly paved track had to be repaired on a daily basis during preparations for the inaugural World 600. *CMS Archives.*

On May 19, 1960, it was announced the speedway couldn't be completed in time for the scheduled date on Memorial Day weekend. The race was reset for June 19, 1960, the only open date on the Grand National (now Sprint Cup) schedule. However, before the speedway could be completed, contractor W. Owen Flowe ordered his crews to halt work in an effort to collect the money he believed he was owed. He placed bulldozers and earthmovers on the last short strip of the track surface that remained unpaved and told his operators to stay on their machines and refuse to move. Turner and Smith brandished weapons and forced the machine operators to leave. The bulldozers were hot-wired and removed from the unfinished track. The men also had to produce enough money at the eleventh hour to place in an escrow account to cover the $106,000 purse.

Tire flaps were placed over the rear tires of the three Petty Plymouths to keep debris from the chunking track from hitting the cars following them during the first World 600. *CMS Archives.*

Paving was completed the morning of the first round of qualifying for the inaugural World 600, leaving it no time to settle. Huge holes in the track surface appeared in the turns. Buck Baker even remarked that a big Chevrolet Impala could have been half hidden in some of the holes. The pavement received patch work daily, and the drivers prepared for the worst. Large screens were placed over the cars' grills and windshields to keep flying rocks and chunks of asphalt out of the radiators. Lee Petty noted that they even put tire flaps over the rear tires of their three Plymouths to keep the debris from flying up into those following them.

During the drivers' meeting, NASCAR executive manager Pat Purcell told the drivers to keep off the dirt apron that separated pit road from the frontstretch. There hadn't been time to plant grass in the area, and NASCAR officials were concerned that a blinding dust storm would occur if cars cut across the area to enter pit road.

A press box had been constructed, but Bob Myers, who was assisting *Charlotte News* motorsports writer Max Muhleman in covering the event, said it wasn't enclosed. He sat in the open-air press box during the race and took notes but returned to the newspaper office in Charlotte to write his story. He described the event as "hilarious."

"The screens on the cars reminded you of cow catchers," Myers noted.

Junior Johnson (6), David Pearson (3), Johnny Allen (46) and Marvin Panch (21) race down the frontstretch in front of an open-air press box. *CMS Archives.*

Sixty cars started the event that took slightly more than five and a half hours to complete before an estimated crowd of 35,462.

Early in the race, Junior Johnson lost control of his Pontiac while exiting turn four. His car skidded into the dusty apron, plowed into the Victory Lane structure that had been placed on the edge of pit road and tore out thirty feet of chain-link fence before stopping on pit road. He received service from his crew before returning to the track.

Soon after Johnson's incident, Lee Petty spun his Plymouth in the same area. He once said that he closed his eyes because of the dust swirling around and when he opened them he had stopped in his pit. The Petty stable had three cars entered in the race—a first for the Level Cross, North Carolina operation—but only one pit crew. Richard Petty noted there was so much tire trouble in the race that one of the Petty cars seemed to always be in the pits. Eventually, the crew just stayed on the pit road side of the wall instead of crossing it prior to and after each stop.

With fewer than fifty laps remaining, it appeared Jack Smith would emerge with the inaugural World 600 victory, but then a chunk of asphalt slammed into his Pontiac's fuel tank, causing gasoline to pour from the car. Smith possessed a five-lap lead at the time, and car owner Bud Moore and mechanic Pop Eargle desperately tried to stop the fuel from gushing out by stuffing rags and steel wool into the opening. When they realized those efforts were futile, Moore began hurriedly searching for a bar of Octagon soap. A lye-based, all-purpose soap that was used for doing laundry before the invention of powder and liquid detergent, Octagon soap was large and soft and, therefore, perfect for plugging the hole. A spectator offered a bar of Camay soap, but it was too small and too hard. Smith continued the race with the leak unsealed.

Smith eventually had to exit the race on lap 352 of 400 and settle for twelfth place. It was a devastating loss for Smith and his Bud Moore–led crew, but it opened the victory door for Joe Lee Johnson of Chattanooga, Tennessee. Johnson was described as "probably the slowest car in the field" by Hill Overton, a Matthews, North Carolina native who had taken leave from his military duty at Fort Eustis to watch the inaugural race. That, however, was apparently what played a key role in Johnson emerging victorious in the race, which Overton described as being like a "war zone" with the chunking and flying asphalt that contributed to the heavy attrition rate. Johnson led the final 48 laps to win $27,150 of the $106,250 purse. Rounding out the top five were, respectively, Johnny Beauchamp, Bobby Johns, Gerald Duke and Buck Baker.

Bruton Smith (center) and Curtis Turner (right) present Joe Lee Johnson with his trophy for winning the inaugural World 600 in 1960. *CMS Archives*.

Junior Johnson and Lee Petty initially finished thirtieth and fifth, but NASCAR disqualified them for making an "improper entrance into the pits." Also disqualified and placed at the end of the finishing order were Richard Petty, Bob Welborn, Paul Lewis and Lennie Page.

The first-ever six-hundred-mile stock car race was in the record books. Even Turner had admitted in his letter in the inaugural event's program that "it hardly seems possible that we have been able to complete the construction of the Speedway in time for the 'World 600.'"

In the letter, Turner told the fans the facilities were "far from complete, but, as you well know, the bad weather during the winter months kept us from putting a lot of the finishing touches" on the track.

"For our next race, I am positive you will find Charlotte Motor Speedway the best racetrack you have ever visited," Turner wrote. "Everything about Charlotte Motor Speedway will be improved upon, and that's a promise!

The track's cafeteria was a popular place with the fans during Charlotte Motor Speedway's opening weekend. *CMS Archives.*

"We will have more seats in the grandstands, more concession stands and more rest rooms and other facilities for you. Too, we will have our sports car course completed by the next race. It will wind around in the infield, giving us a 2½-mile track for other races."

The track president wrote it was a "pleasure" to be associated with the facility's general manager and executive vice-president, Bruton Smith, and he commended the construction contractors for completing a two-year job in about nine months.

Bruton Smith wrote in his letter that was contained in the inaugural World 600 program that to be a part of Charlotte Motor Speedway and to be associated with Curtis Turner was "even more gratifying" than to be part of stock car racing's growth. He, too, noted that numerous improvements were planned, and when fans returned for the next event, they might "hardly recognize the place." He also cited the slogan he and Turner had adopted: "Charlotte Motor Speedway…it's for everyone."

Despite insurmountable odds, Curtis Turner and Bruton Smith had done what many believed impossible: constructed a one-and-a-half-mile speedway on horrible terrain in less than a year, opened it and conducted a race. They had magnificent plans for their speedway, but there was one major problem that stood in their way: a tremendous amount of debt incurred during the track's construction. Ticket sales covered the immediate loans for the race's purse, but there was a long line of creditors demanding to be paid.

CHAPTER TWO

FINANCIAL WOES

D espite the issues with the track's surface during the inaugural World
600 and the mounting debt, Curtis Turner and Bruton Smith pressed
forward, scheduling the track's second NASCAR event for October 16, 1960.
Six days prior to the event, NASCAR president Bill France Sr., a former
race car driver himself, inspected the track and declared it wasn't dangerous.
France checked the speedway due to a wreck that destroyed Tom Pistone's
car during a practice session. Rex White was at the shake-down session with
Pistone and discontinued his test, blaming the track for Pistone's accident.
Initially, speedway officials threatened to decline White's entry due to his
remarks about the track's surface. However, his entry was accepted, and White
eventually finished sixth in the October race's fifty-car field.

Even though White wrapped up the 1960 championship in the inaugural
National 400, it was winner Speedy Thompson who stole the headlines.
Thompson hadn't won a race since 1958, and his last full season on the
circuit had been 1959. The veteran secured his nineteenth career victory
in the four-hundred-mile event by avoiding a series of tire problems and
crashes. Thompson assumed the number one position in his Wood Brothers
Ford after leader Fireball Roberts's Pontiac blew a tire and hit the wall on lap
233 of the 267-lap race. The Monroe, North Carolina driver led the final 35
laps to finish a lap ahead of runner-up Richard Petty.

Rounding out the top five were, respectively, Ned Jarrett, Bobby Johns and
Junior Johnson.

The Charlotte Motor Speedway track surface didn't come apart during
the facility's second race, but the event was marred by a spectacular crash

Brothers Glen (center) and Leonard Wood (right) meet with a NASCAR official. The Wood Brothers fielded the car that won the first fall race ever held at Charlotte Motor Speedway. *CMS Archives.*

involving Lennie Page and Don O'Dell. On lap ninety-three, Page's Thunderbird hit the wall and bounced into the path of O'Dell's Pontiac. The vicious hit knocked Page unconscious and left him with a concussion, several broken ribs and a deep puncture in his neck. *National Speed Sport News* editor and publisher Chris Economaki, who was taking photos for his newspaper, hurriedly removed his shirt, tightly wrapped Page's neck with it and provided treatment until an ambulance arrived.

Despite the large field of NASCAR's star drivers, attendance at the track's October race dropped to fewer than thirty thousand, a fact that only added to the facility's financial woes.

Curtis Turner had approached the Teamsters Union about an $800,000 loan to bail the speedway out of debt after the inaugural World 600.

Formed in 1903, the Teamsters had become the largest union in the United States by 1940. Presidents Dave Beck (1952–57) and Jimmy Hoffa (1957–71) shaped the Teamsters into a strongly centralized union capable of

An ambulance was stationed inside one of the speedway's turns during the 1960s. *CMS Archives.*

negotiating nationwide freight-hauling agreements. At that time, the union possessed great bargaining power due to its size and the threat it carried of halting shipments of essential goods. However, during this era the union's magnitude also provided some officials with the opportunity to violently pressure small employers or profit, in partnership with organized crime, from the manipulation of union pension funds. Accountant and attorney William R. Rabin, a confidante of many people, including Teamster boss Jimmy Hoffa, was hired to set up Charlotte Motor Speedway's books. Rabin played a key role in persuading each creditor to give the speedway's management more time to repay its debts. He also was the liaison between Turner and the Teamsters in their original discussions. In return for the six-figure loan, Turner was to unionize the drivers and get parimutuel betting in the sport. Turner temporarily abandoned the idea after talking with some drivers.

Even though the speedway was slowly paying off its debt, when it celebrated its first anniversary, it wasn't progressing fast enough for its creditors and stockholders. In early June 1961, slightly more than a week after the second World 600, the track's board of directors held a meeting to which Turner wasn't invited—technically a violation of North Carolina law. A stormy meeting ensued the next day. Curtis Turner was ousted as president and Bruton Smith resigned as vice-president. Charlotte-area businessmen and stockholders in the racetrack Allan Nance and C.D. "Duke" Ellington took their places. Nance was elected the speedway's president while Ellington was elected vice-president and appointed general manager. Smith was temporarily kept on as the track's promotion director, but before 1961 had ended, he also was gone from the speedway.

Smith attempted to maintain possession of the track via the court system, but he said his attorneys filed the wrong paperwork.

"I found out in New York about a corporate reorganization," Smith explained during a May 2009 press conference in the speedway's infield media center. "There had never been one filed in this state [North Carolina] at that time. The lawyers I had were kind of stupid. They didn't know what I was trying to do. They filed Chapter 10 instead of Chapter 11. Chapter 10 is where a trustee is in control."

The fact that the wrong documents were filed resulted in the court taking over and appointing who would operate the speedway instead of Smith retaining control and the racetrack undergoing reorganization.

Smith eventually left North Carolina, but Turner decided he would return to the Teamsters and accept their original proposal in an effort to regain control of the speedway he and Smith had built. At the time, the Teamsters wanted to unionize professional athletes in various sports, and money was no object in their effort to accomplish the feat.

The week of August 7, 1961, Turner, along with other people involved in the motorsports industry, met in Chicago with Teamster officials Nick Torzeski and Harold Gibbons. Torzeski was involved with the organizing of professional athletes, while Gibbons was Hoffa's administrative aide. Without fanfare, several drivers from NASCAR and the United States Auto Club (USAC) met and formed the Federation of Professional Athletes (FPA). They said that their purpose was to form a union that represented all professional race car drivers, and their objectives for members were: upgraded facilities for drivers and the speedways, including shower and lounge facilities; better purses; pension plans; a scholarship fund for children of deceased members; and more adequate insurance coverage. It wasn't mentioned, however, that the FPA would bring parimutuel betting to auto racing.

In addition to Turner, other NASCAR drivers reported at the meeting were Fireball Roberts and Tim Flock. Turner told Torzeski and Gibbons that in exchange for $850,000, which would bail Charlotte Motor Speedway out of its impending bankruptcy, he would lead the effort to unionize stock car drivers. Turner located the fledgling union's office in the Nissen Building in Winston-Salem, North Carolina. A statement he released on August 8,

1961, said a majority of the Grand National drivers had signed applications and paid the $10 initiation dues for membership in the FPA.

Curtis Turner's statement made NASCAR president Bill France Sr. irate. He replied with the now famous remark that no known Teamster member could compete in a NASCAR race and he would use a pistol to enforce it. The Grand National Series (now Sprint Cup) had a race scheduled for August 9, 1961, in Winston-Salem's Bowman-Gray Stadium. France immediately traveled to that Piedmont city and met with the drivers in a vacant building near the stadium. It was then that France informed the competitors that before he would allow the union to be "stuffed down" his throat, he would plow up Daytona International Speedway and plant corn in the infield. He then levied a lifetime suspension against Turner, Flock and Roberts for "conduct detrimental to auto racing." France also noted that auto racing was one of the few sports that had never had a scandal and "we'll fight this union to the hilt."

In a prepared statement that France released in response to one that Turner had sent to many daily newspapers and racing tabloids explaining the FPA's position, France said he didn't know why the drivers became

> associated with movements [that] can only hurt and degrade our sport and injure the people and organization that helped them grow. But I do know that organized gambling would be bad for our sport—and would spill innocent blood on our race track—I'll fight it to the end! And with the help of all decent auto racing people and their fans, we will lick it. I know and believe that trade unions have a good place in the American way of life. However, the kind those boys are working with can't do anything but hurt racing, and all the nice folks who have been building our great sport.

While Curtis Turner and Bill France Sr. continued their verbal sparring, NASCAR vice-president Ed Otto remained calm. Among his many statements he noted that New York's appellate court had ruled in 1951 that race car drivers were not "employees" but contestants and independent contractors. This ruling directly affected workmen's compensation in the sport. Because the competitors were independent contractors, NASCAR wasn't required by law to provide workmen's compensation insurance. This was one fact Otto cited in noting that the "relationships of the people involved in automobile racing do not constitute a proper basis for unionization."

Fireball Roberts resigned from the Federation of Professional Athletes on August 11, 1961, and many of the other drivers followed suit. In fact, all of

Fireball Roberts lost his life due to complications from the severe burns that he suffered in a three-car wreck at Charlotte Motor Speedway. *CMS Archives.*

the drivers except for Turner and Tim Flock returned to Bill France Sr.'s fold. The two drivers filed several lawsuits, including one for reinstatement in NASCAR under Florida's right to work law. They also sought $300,000 in actual and punitive damages with a request for a temporary injunction. Circuit judge Robert E. Wingfield dismissed the temporary injunction request on January 13, 1962. A few days later, Turner's attorneys advised him to drop the entire suit. It turns out the Teamsters couldn't legally make a loan to a company they were attempting to organize.

Flock never raced again in NASCAR, but several years later, he would work in Charlotte Motor Speedway's marketing department, promoting the facility at various races on the then Winston Cup circuit. Flock and wife Frances were a favorite with the fans and remained with CMS until he lost his battle with cancer on March 31, 1998.

With his suspension from NASCAR upheld, Turner headed for Hollywood, where he had been invited to meet with scriptwriters who were interested in a movie about his career. A movie deal never materialized, but

Turner enjoyed the parties. In fact, when he returned to Charlotte, he told his buddies that Frank Sinatra really knew how to "put on a party." Turner competed in non-NASCAR events, including the Pikes Peak Hill Climb, but as soon as he was notified in 1965 that his suspension had been lifted, he wasted little time in returning. Turner and his fans were ecstatic that he was racing once again in NASCAR. On October 31, 1965, the forty-one-year-old Turner out-dueled a twenty-six-year-old Cale Yarborough to win the inaugural American 500 at the new one-mile speedway in Rockingham, North Carolina. It was his last major racing triumph. No matter how diligent his efforts, Curtis Turner never regained control of his beloved Charlotte Motor Speedway. He and friend and professional golfer Clarence King died in a plane crash on October 4, 1970, in Punxsutawney, Pennsylvania.

While Turner had attempted to obtain funding via the Teamsters so that he could regain control of Charlotte Motor Speedway, the track's debts had continued to mount. By December 1961, there were more than $1 million in outstanding liens from creditors. The track's management staved off a foreclosure sale, and the track was placed under Chapter 10 of the Federal Bankruptcy Act. Judge J.B. Craven Jr. appointed Robert "Red" Robinson the trustee and gave him until March 1962 to develop a plan that would satisfy the speedway's creditors.

It was at this time that Richard Howard, a personable, astute businessman from Denver, North Carolina, came into the picture. A stockholder in Charlotte Motor Speedway, Howard was known for his multiple successful small businesses. In March 1962, A.C. Goines, a member of the speedway's original board of directors, and Howard raised $254,000 from stockholders in an effort to match a promised $300,000 loan to halt foreclosure. The two men led a stockholders' meeting in a building at Park Road Shopping Center in south Charlotte in an effort to make up the $46,000 shortfall. Howard possessed a tremendous understanding of people, so he figured it would be a good move if he made the first contribution, one that totaled $5,000. Within two hours, the two men had surpassed their goal with a total of $301,510.

Despite this achievement, the CMS management still had a sizeable amount of debt to pay. Four months later, trustee Red Robinson again requested Judge J.B. Craven give the stockholders more time to reorganize. Craven granted the request, and by April 1963, $740,376 in debts had been paid to twenty secured creditors. When the track emerged from bankruptcy, Craven appointed A.C. Goines the speedway's president, Duke Ellington its executive vice-president and Richard Howard its vice-president and general manager. Craven named Goines and Howard to their respective positions in an effort to get the speedway solvent because at the time, the men were the facility's two biggest stockholders, explained Bob Moore, the motorsports writer for the *Charlotte Observer* during much of Howard's tenure at the track.

Howard, who later became the financially ailing track's president, also was the type of person the speedway really needed.

"He was a very smart man, very outgoing," Moore noted. "He got the fans and drivers to come down, made sure NASCAR was getting the sanctioning fees. He had to make sure there was no problem with NASCAR so it wouldn't pull the sanction. He also made sure the local media

Richard Howard rescued Charlotte Motor Speedway from bankruptcy. *Pal Parker Photography.*

were kept informed with what was going on. Every decision he made during that time was aimed at getting [CMS] out of bankruptcy."

Having grown up on a farm in Sherrills Ford, North Carolina, north of Charlotte during the Great Depression, Howard had a thorough understanding of conservative financial practices. He also possessed a mind that was constantly "churning…always trying to think of a way to get ahead in life," said Howard's son, Rick.

One of four children, Richard Stowe Howard was born December 7, 1924, in Sherrills Ford. Now a popular area on Lake Norman, it was a small farming community for most of Howard's life. In fact, the only thing that ever drew him away from his roots was World War II. Immediately after graduating high school at age seventeen, Howard joined the marine corps. He was sent to the Pacific and "got shot up pretty bad" in the Battle of Okinawa. After his discharge from the marines, Howard returned home, married his high school sweetheart (Eathel White), settled in Denver, North Carolina—a short distance from Sherrills Ford—and obtained a job in a cotton mill. He also worked for a short time at a "machine-shop-like" business in Mooresville, North Carolina.

Howard, however, was always searching for that next good business deal. This time it was selling furniture on nights and weekends at a friend's hardware store in Conover, North Carolina. The side business was doing so well that he decided to add furniture and an appliance line to the hardware store full time. Howard soon decided that he would construct a furniture store beside his Denver home, and Howard's Furniture was born.

"He was there all the time," son Rick Howard said. He continued:

> *We were going over there all times of the night because someone's refrigerator would blow up or their washing machine or dryer would quit working. It was the stuff people needed, and he didn't want them to go without the stuff they needed. It became a life-long experience for the family.*
>
> *We had accounts at the furniture store that went unpaid. I was an accountant and so was my grandfather. I'd say, "Dad, we need to collect this money." He'd say, "You know. Those people need it worse than us. They'll pay us when they can." He wasn't a bad businessman. He just felt people needed something when they needed it. He cared about everybody and he could talk to anybody.*

That ability to converse with anyone, from the corporate executive to the millworker, paid huge dividends for Howard as he diligently worked to rescue Charlotte Motor Speedway from the heavy debt in which it was drowning. At the time, no one would give the speedway any credit. Bob Myers, motorsports writer for the *Charlotte News* during Howard's years at the speedway, noted that track controller and secretary-treasurer Guy Charles once told him they couldn't even obtain credit for a keg of nails.

Despite the odds, Richard Howard still managed to develop good, strong relationships with NASCAR president Bill France Sr., Firestone representative H.A. "Humpy" Wheeler, R.J. Reynolds Tobacco Company's Ralph Seagraves and veteran driver and team owner Junior Johnson, just to mention a few. It was those relationships that really paid dividends.

"I knew they didn't have any money down there, and I would help them as much as I could," Wheeler said in regards to his days with Firestone Tire and Rubber Company. "At that time, Firestone was the biggest company in racing as far as spending money and stuff. We had a signage program at the tracks, things like that."

Wheeler, a Belmont, North Carolina native who had known Richard oward since his teenage years, noted that in addition to the track's mounting

NASCAR president Bill France Sr. (left) and Richard Howard developed a strong relationship, one that helped Charlotte Motor Speedway survive. *Pal Parker Photography.*

debt, the energetic Howard had to contend with two major problems in the speedway's infield. One was a huge rock mound that blocked the view of the second turn for the fans sitting in the frontstretch grandstands. The other was a giant, sixty-foot-deep hole in the infield near the third turn.

In the 1960s, the gas pumps where fuel was obtained for the race cars didn't even have a roof over them. *CMS Archives.*

"The third turn was built just like you build a dam today," Wheeler said. He explained:

> *They kept adding dirt, and when they finished adding dirt, it was 130 feet of vertical fill. They put dirt behind it to create the road and also safety wise so if a car went out of the track, it wouldn't drop thirteen stories; it would go only about six. [Once the turn was built] they didn't have enough dirt left over to fill that giant hole.*
>
> *Richard Howard is the one who figured out how to fill up the hole. He made a deal with the City of Charlotte to bring garbage in and fill that hole in. That was a masterful, creative idea because Richard*

is sitting there trying to run the track with no money and paying off debtors.

It truly appeared Charlotte Motor Speedway had received a second chance and was on the right path to financial recovery. Then it suddenly became the site of one of the sport's most tragic accidents. The date was May 24, 1964. It was the World 600's eighth lap when Junior Johnson's and Ned Jarrett's Fords spun off the second turn. Fireball Roberts was attempting to miss the spinning cars when his Ford spun backward into the edge of a concrete wall on the backstretch. On impact, Roberts's car exploded, flipped and began burning. Jarrett's car spun to a stop near Roberts's Ford and was quickly engulfed in the flames. Jarrett jumped from his burning car and

Lee Petty's (center) cars finished first and second in the 1964 World 600, with Jim Paschal (left) winning and Petty's son Richard placing second. *CMS Archives.*

ran to Roberts's aid. Roberts, who had managed to half free himself, was screaming for his friend to pull him from the inferno. There were no fuel cells and fire retardant uniforms at the time, and Roberts's asthma kept him from using a fire retardant chemical on his clothing. The Florida native was airlifted to Charlotte Memorial Hospital in "extremely critical" condition due to his severe burns. He remained hospitalized until he succumbed to blood poisoning and pneumonia on July 2, 1964.

The World 600 that cost Roberts his life was won by Jim Paschal, who defeated Petty Enterprises teammate Richard Petty by four laps.

Later that year, tragedy came to the speedway again when Jimmy Pardue lost his life during a tire test. In these years, the inner liner for race tires was still under development, so there was still a safety issue when a tire blew. Pardue's Plymouth blew a tire entering the third turn, plowed through the track's guardrail and tumbled down the steep embankment.

These tragedies at the track as well as the Chrysler boycott of NASCAR's Grand National (now Sprint Cup) Series in 1965 and Ford's withdrawal from the circuit in 1966 all served to lower attendance figures, the latter two because they affected many of the fans' favorite drivers. Despite these setbacks, Howard continued to use his good business sense to methodically rid Charlotte Motor Speedway of its financial problems. On June 1, 1967, Howard took nearly $300,000 to a bank in Newton, North Carolina, to clear the track of its remaining debts. Eighteen days later, the heavy-set Howard held a mortgage burning for speedway officials and invited guests.

"If it wasn't for Richard Howard, Charlotte Motor Speedway would have gone belly up. There wouldn't be a Charlotte Motor Speedway today," said former *Charlotte Observer* motorsports writer Bob Moore. "Actually, if it wasn't for Richard, there wouldn't be an Atlanta (Motor Speedway) or Charlotte. In 1969 and '70, Atlanta had huge financial problems, and Richard went down there and got them out of that hole, too."

(Atlanta's financial woes came in the summer of 1970, when American Raceways Incorporated [ARI], which operated the Atlanta track under a management contract that was tied to a loan agreement, failed to post the prize money for the August 2 Dixie 500. ARI hadn't paid Investors Diversified Services a $100,000 quarterly note, and Larry LoPatin, a Detroit financier who headed ARI, notified NASCAR president Bill France Sr. that the race might not be held because he had not posted ARI's $89,600 portion of the purse. Four days before the Dixie 500, France removed it from the schedule. Richard Howard took it upon himself to post that portion of the purse.)

"He loved the sport and the people in it," Rick Howard said about his father. "He touched every part of it. I think he left it better than he found it. He died loving the sport."

Even though Howard—who weighed more than three hundred pounds for most of his life and died April 28, 1998, of congestive heart failure—returned Charlotte Motor Speedway to profitability, he was able to make only minor, if any, improvements to the speedway and surrounding property during his time at the helm due to the tremendous debt hanging over the facility. Four months after the mortgage burning, very little had changed since the speedway opened in 1960. The large, two-story yellow wooden farmhouse still served as the track's office with tickets sold on race day at walkup windows on one side of the house. The small cemeteries created by the original property

The yellow two-story farmhouse located at the speedway's entrance served as the facility's first office building. *CMS Archives.*

owner remained, as did numerous large shade trees. The steep, concrete steps with iron railing down the center that led from the parking area to the grandstands were crumbling. Parking was relegated to dirt lots and fields, with traffic control sorely lacking even though a four-lane highway ran in front of the speedway. It wasn't uncommon for race morning traffic to come to a standstill, blocking one side of Highway 29 for at least five miles. And a three-hour wait to get onto the main road from the parking lot after an event wasn't unusual either.

Moore recalled the strain that the bankruptcy situation put on the speedway:

When Richard took over, it took them a lot of time before they were able to spend money on repairing what needed to be repaired. He spent the money on what he felt he needed to do to attract the crowds to make the money to pay the bills. Their first priority was to get out from underneath the bankruptcy judge. If the bankruptcy judge at any time had told them they weren't making any headway and not paying off their bills that would have been it. They had to make sure they kept the track alive. Everything they did they had to get approved by the bankruptcy court. In any bankruptcy deal, the court can pull the plug if they don't think you're heading in the right direction. Richard had to be a big sales person because when he said he wanted to spend a certain amount of money on something, the court would want to know why. He had to be a salesman not only to bring in the race fans but also to keep the court happy.

Howard's dedication paid off. By 1972, Charlotte Motor Speedway had been out of bankruptcy for nearly five years. Two concrete tower grandstands had been constructed, and multicolored roofs at the back of the ground-level frontstretch grandstands provided shade to the top two or three rows. The Ford Tower was at the entrance to the first turn above the Ford Grandstand while the Chrysler Tower was above the Chrysler Grandstand at the fourth turn exit. The small press box was at the start-finish line atop the last row of the General Motors Grandstand.

Even though improvements to the facility were moving slowly, it was Howard's ability to promote that triggered interest in the speedway and its upcoming races.

"He was way out in front of the curve," Rick Howard said about his father. "His country upbringing, his business savvy was perfect for a promoter."

Howard began bringing Indy Car drivers, such as A.J. Foyt, Mario Andretti and Johnny Rutherford, in for the October races. He helped some

A WBT radio reporter interviews Fred Lorenzen. *CMS Archives.*

of the smaller teams, those that often ran in the back of the field, by paying them deal money. Moore noted he also reduced ticket prices, developed special promotions and escorted drivers to local newspapers and TV stations for interviews.

"He was a big-time promoter long before Humpy [Wheeler] and Bruton [Smith]," Moore said. "He would go on two or three mini media tours and take two or three drivers to Spartanburg, Columbia, Greensboro, Winston-Salem and High Point to generate as much publicity as possible."

"Richard didn't mind spending money," Moore continued. "He understood that to make money, you have to spend money. He was frugal in

Drivers prepare for the start of a race in the 1960s at Charlotte Motor Speedway with a pace lap. *CMS Archives.*

that [he knew] they had to watch their pennies because of the bankruptcy court, but he also realized there were cases where you had to spend extra money, and he didn't mind spending it."

That included fielding a race team. Howard knew people attending the races in that era were car-make, not driver, fans, Moore noted, and he knew in order to fill the grandstands he had to have good Chevrolet, Ford, Plymouth and Dodge teams competing at his track. Therefore, when 1971 arrived, Howard was concerned about attendance for that year's World 600 due to the auto manufacturers having withdrawn their financial support from the sport. Several of the top independents also had quit due to no longer having good equipment. Only three or four teams were able to obtain new parts. That's when Howard decided it was the perfect time for a competitive Chevrolet to return to NASCAR, something that had been absent since 1963.

In March 1971, Howard said publicly he wanted a Chevrolet with the potential to win the World 600 in the field, and he wanted Junior Johnson to build and drive it. By early April, however, Johnson had decided that he didn't want to drive the car, so he and Howard arranged for him to build one, something the speedway head still viewed as a good promotional tool. Charlie Glotzbach was selected as the driver, and when it came time for him

Brothers Eddie, Donnie (center) and Bobby Allison (right) first visited Charlotte Motor Speedway in the 1960s. Bobby would later win six races at the track and Donnie three. *CMS Archives.*

to perform, the Indiana driver produced. He earned the pole for the circuit's longest race with a speed of 157.788 miles per hour, and Howard didn't have an attendance problem on race day with an estimated seventy-eight thousand fans coming to watch the event.

During the race, Glotzbach provided Chevrolet fans with a reason to cheer and Ford fans an opportunity to boo. He led four times for 87 laps and was running second on lap 234, when he hit the frontstretch wall due to the lane being taken by a slower car. Within minutes, Howard appeared in the press box and announced Johnson would build another Chevrolet for the National 500 in October. Johnson entered the potent Chevrolet wherever promoters were willing to pay for it. The new team competed in thirteen races during the season's second half for a total of fifteen races that year. In those fifteen outings, the organization collected one victory, four poles and seven top fives.

The team enjoyed its most successful season in 1972, when Bobby Allison piloted the Coca-Cola-sponsored Chevrolet to 10 victories, 25 top fives, 27 top tens and 11 poles in 31 races. Howard's team competed in at least 1 race each season from 1970 to 1976. The last year he financed a team was 1981, when Elliott Forbes-Robinson competed in 10 events. During Richard Howard's tenure as a car owner, his teams competed in 110 races, won 21, posted 60 top fives and 71 top tens and earned 22 poles.

Stunt drivers perform a pre-race show. *CMS Archives.*

Rick Howard remembered:

> *Dad was always trying to figure out ways to put more butts in the seats...he would try anything, and most of it he made work. He had some really good people. You have to put the right people together* [to make anything work].
>
> *I think Dad would have been successful during the good times and now. He had that connection with people, and I'm talking about all people, from media to other track owners, race fans, drivers, manufacturers. He just had a knack for having a relationship with everybody.*

In 1970, the National Motorsports Press Association presented Richard Howard with the Myers Brothers Award, an honor given to an individual or a group that has made outstanding contributions to the sport of stock car racing. The man dubbed the mom-and-pop millionaire by the media had rescued Charlotte Motor Speedway from bankruptcy and turned it into a viable business. Now he looked forward to improving the facility and growing attendance. However, there was a major change on the horizon, one that would blindside Howard and drastically alter the course he had charted for the one-and-a-half-mile track.

CHAPTER THREE

REGAINING CONTROL

While Richard Howard was diligently and methodically working to remove Charlotte Motor Speedway from bankruptcy, Bruton Smith was implementing the plan that he had carefully designed to deliver the track he and Turner had built back into his hands.

After being ousted as the speedway's general manager in 1961, Smith briefly operated a short dirt track in Concord, North Carolina, before moving to Denver, Colorado, to work at a friend and business associate's Ford dealership. He eventually left Colorado, moved to Rockford, Illinois, and joined the Ford Dealer Development program. By 1969, Smith had acquired his first auto dealership. Five years later, he owned a network of ten dealerships and two insurance companies. With the money Smith obtained from his businesses, he quietly began buying Charlotte Motor Speedway stock, something the track's management team never imagined would occur. Former *Charlotte Observer* motorsports writer Bob Moore said Smith was paying above market value for the stock. He also noted that Smith had one condition for the person from whom he purchased the stock: don't identify who had acquired it to anyone. By the mid-1970s, Smith was the speedway's majority stockholder.

"The idea of Bruton coming back never occurred to [the CMS management]," Moore said. "When Bruton left, no one thought he was coming back. All of a sudden, he shows up, and he's a major stockholder. He caught them—the management team and the board of directors—by surprise. They didn't believe Bruton had enough money to do it."

Once Smith became the speedway's majority stockholder, he began putting allies on the track's board of directors. Finally, he had enough of his people on the board to control it.

"[Of course] in order to do that he had to buy out Richard Howard," said Humpy Wheeler, who had entered the promotion business at age thirteen, when he organized Saturday afternoon bicycle races so that he wouldn't have to mow lawns and deliver papers. Wheeler remembered:

> *It was a bitter fight there that lasted for a long time. It lasted for two or three years after I went to work at the speedway.*
>
> *When he bought Richard's stock, as part of it, he asked Richard to step down. Richard said he would, but he made a deal with Bruton that he would stay on for a year. So Bruton brought everyone in and Richard would give him some advice and counseling.*

It was now 1975, and Smith and Wheeler were about to embark on a journey that would last more than thirty years: a business partnership that would transform the speedway into an industry leader for fan, media and corporate amenities; host pre-race shows and historical events, both good and bad; and have numerous disagreements. Every day would be an adventure for the two men, one that sometimes would leave them at odds with NASCAR, TV networks, the series' sponsors and, on occasion, the competitors and each other. Both enjoyed developing and building. In fact, Smith often described himself as a frustrated builder. However, as Wheeler noted, Smith's ideas were more "palatial" than his.

"I said one time his was the Ritz Carlton, and I was the Holiday Inn," Wheeler noted.

The business relationship that lasted for decades got off to a rocky start many years earlier. At the time, Howard Augustine "Humpy" Wheeler Jr., a Belmont, North Carolina native who was born October 23, 1938, was a teenager and Smith was the race promoter at the Charlotte Fairgrounds. Wheeler was the writer of weekly columns for the *Belmont Banner* and *Mount Holly News*, and he had gone to the Fairgrounds to produce an article. He introduced himself to Smith and showed him his North Carolina Press card. Smith refused to honor the press card and wouldn't grant Wheeler access to the event.

"So I never wrote another word about any of the races he was running, which was kind of weird because back in those days, there were two TV stations and the *Charlotte Observer*," Wheeler said. "Then there were weekly papers, which

Despite the tough working conditions that existed in the garage during the 1960s, the competitors maintained a sense of humor. *CMS Archives.*

later on when I was promoting dirt [track races], I depended on the weekly papers to stir up all of the millworkers who were the fans."

Wheeler, a strong-willed, hardworking man of Scots-Irish ancestry—who at age ten was hitchhiking to the old Charlotte Speedway so he could watch the races—eventually got over his initial clash with Smith.

"He didn't know me from a hay seed then," Wheeler commented.

It wasn't until Wheeler was a student at the University of South Carolina and Smith was operating a short track in the early 1960s that the two men became acquainted with each other. After graduating from college, Wheeler worked at WBTV in Charlotte for a short time before quitting his job to take over the operation of Robinwood Speedway, a dirt track in Gastonia, North Carolina. On the side, he also handled advertising for the bankrupt

Charlotte Motor Speedway. By then, Bruton Smith had turned to selling cars and operating Concord Speedway, a dirt track off U.S. Highway 29 that was within ten miles of the track he and Turner had built.

"He had a partner with him, and they were selling stock," Wheeler recalled. "They were going to make that a super duper dirt track, and they had already spent quite a bit of money on it. He wanted me to go to work for him. I didn't want to do that because I was doing fine with my track."

Wheeler and Smith would occasionally bump into each other. However, there wasn't any competition between them because their tracks were about forty miles apart, and in the 1960s, people didn't travel as far as they do now to attend short-track races.

The two men left North Carolina about the same time, Wheeler said. Smith headed for Denver, Colorado, to work at a friend's Ford dealership, and Wheeler left for employment with Firestone Tire and Rubber Company in Ohio. Wheeler, who encountered Smith one day at an Indy Car race in Phoenix, said they kept in touch with each other but not on a regular basis.

Once Smith regained control of Charlotte Motor Speedway, he asked Wheeler about becoming the facility's general manager. At the time, Wheeler was working for the Ervin Company, a large real estate developer, and he didn't know if he wanted to re-enter the motorsports industry. Wheeler had left racing in 1970, when Firestone withdrew from the sport, saying 1964–70 had been a "very, very traumatic period" for him.

"With the terrible, terrible amount of death and destruction that had gone on, speed had way, way outrun safety in Indy Cars, NASCAR and Formula One," Wheeler explained. "So many friends of mine had gotten killed. I had pulled three or four guys out of race cars who were dead."

Wheeler also had to identify Eddie Sachs after the horrendous fiery crash on the second lap of the 1964 Indianapolis 500 that killed Sachs and Dave MacDonald, involved five other drivers and left three of them injured, one with burns over 75 percent of his body.

"It was really, really beginning to wear on me," Wheeler admitted. "At the same time, the period from 1970 to 1975 was relatively peaceful as far as driver death and injury were concerned. So that gave me hope because of the fuel cell and the [tire] inner liner that we had addressed the problem. I knew it would come back; it always does."

Wheeler had other concerns with the industry, as well:

Another thing that made me think about doing something else and getting out of the racing business was that no one was making much

The first three races conducted at Charlotte Motor Speedway each had a field of at least fifty cars. *CMS Archives.*

money. There just wasn't any money in it for anybody, and there were a lot of risks. Risks for people getting in it, and risks for drivers as far as their safety was concerned. At the same time, I did see a bright future for it if we could get our act together and ever get some major sponsors besides automobile companies.

Those, however, weren't the only factors weighing on Wheeler's mind as he debated for three weeks whether or not to accept Smith's offer. The track's condition concerned him. It needed a great deal of work, and he knew it had never really produced terribly competitive races because it was so narrow.

"You got down to forty feet of width in some of the corners," Wheeler explained. "The dirt track we built was sixty-five feet wide. I was concerned

Richard Petty uses a tire for a seat in the original Charlotte Motor Speedway garage. *CMS Archives.*

about the length of the track being one and a half miles, how competitive the races could be. The six hundred miles was another factor."

Also, it bothered Wheeler that at that time, the only asphalt on the original 550 acres was the actual track. There was none in the pit area, only a concrete pad that the cars sat on with a little Florida parking lot roof on it. The scoreboard was one Wheeler had gotten installed when he was out of racing and handling some consulting work for a California-based scoreboard building company named Conrac. One addition consisting of about 1,200 seats had been installed, and Wheeler's brother-in-law Jack Spain had been responsible for it. No chair seats existed, the press box was extremely small and there were only eight VIP suites "and not much to them." The huge hole in the infield between the third and fourth turns still existed, even though Richard Howard had contracted with the City of Charlotte to use it as a landfill when he managed the track. Also still standing was the big rock hill that blocked the view of the second turn for those sitting on the frontstretch. (Eventually that hill was removed, and the rock finished filling the large hole in the infield.)

Water was also an issue. The speedway sat on a series of about thirty wells that fit into a main line, and there were three storage tanks for water.

"Being on a well and septic system for a racetrack is definitely not the way to go unless it's a short track," Wheeler commented.

The track did have seventy-two thousand seats, but some of them were on the backstretch and that wasn't acceptable.

Wheeler recalled:

> *When you added it all up together, I think probably the biggest thing that got me was our reputation in Cabarrus County. It was awful! It stemmed back to that rock concert they'd had in 1974. They never did figure out how many people were there because halfway through the first day, people broke the fence down. Thousands of people poured into the place, and they were completely unprepared for it. The Cabarrus Sheriff's Department was overwhelmed. So was the hospital, mostly with drug overdoses. [The City of] Concord was mad because of what it did to the hospital and the jail. The sheriff's department was mad because of having to put up with it. In short, they were pretty much against the speedway.*
>
> *We had a lot going against us at the time. Also, that was right at the period when racing hadn't quite taken off yet. You could see the seeds of it growing. I instinctively knew it would bloom if we could ever find a way to borrow money, which we absolutely could not do at that time. As far as getting money to spend, it was impossible.*

Despite his reservations, Wheeler finally accepted Smith's offer and agreed to start Labor Day weekend of 1975. Smith had told Wheeler that he could begin developing the speedway because hardly any money had been spent on it due to the bankruptcy and after the October five-hundred-mile race, he would become the general manager.

"Even though Richard [Howard] and Bruton had a bitter relationship for a long time, Richard agreed to stay through the 1976 World 600 even though I was the general manager," Wheeler said. "I told Richard I really needed his advice and counsel. I always had a tremendous amount of respect for

Companies selling their products to competitors in the 1960s used the vehicle in which they traveled for their office. *CMS Archives.*

him. I had known him since I was a teenager when he was selling furniture in Denver. Thank goodness he agreed to stay. He helped me tremendously getting through that period of time."

Never one to dwell on negative issues, Richard Howard maintained his love of racing once he left the track but turned the bulk of his attention to his numerous mom-and-pop businesses and his slow-pitch softball teams that set the gold standard in the sport. During a fifteen-year period, his Howard's Furniture–Western Steer men's softball teams captured twelve national championships, while a women's team and a youth team captured one each. Howard even constructed a softball field behind his furniture store. He also owned restaurants, car washes, bowling alleys and a bakery and a ham curing business and sold restaurant equipment and insurance.

"You name it, and he probably tried it," son Rick Howard said.

While Howard was moving away from the speedway, Wheeler found himself facing two monumental tasks: trying to get media outside the Charlotte area to cover events at the track and selling tickets to the 1976 World 600. Other than the *Charlotte Observer* and the Associated Press, the track received only lip service "at best" from the Raleigh *News and Observer* and the *Columbia State*.

"When you got out of hitting range to the *Atlanta Journal*, the *Philadelphia Enquirer*, the *New York Times*, you just didn't get anything," Wheeler noted. He continued to explain:

> *In general, it was pretty tough to get publicity and pretty much impossible to get any in advance. Getting it in advance is when you needed it because you needed to sell the tickets. That had to be attacked big time. We had a lot of work to do with media across the Carolinas because my contention has always been if you're not big at home, you're not going to be big in New York, Chicago or L.A. At that time, we were locked into a southern mentality. It was a southern sport. Most of the drivers were from the South, primarily the Carolinas.*

With the 1976 World 600 fast approaching, ticket sales were extremely sluggish. The media and the majority of the fans had little interest in Charlotte Motor Speedway and the World 600. They were focused on Indianapolis, where Janet Guthrie was attempting to become the first woman to qualify for the historic five-hundred-mile May classic. Previously, women had never been allowed to enter the Indianapolis 500, but Guthrie was relentless and had passed her rookie test. Officials had no choice but to allow her an attempt to qualify for the race. Even the *Charlotte Observer* was giving more column inches to Guthrie than it was the upcoming six-hundred-mile stock car race in the newspaper's own backyard.

"You could go to downtown Concord, and people would be talking about Janet Guthrie, 'that woman,'" Wheeler noted.

At that time, practice began at Indianapolis the first of May and occurred daily until race week. Having spent the month of May at Indianapolis when he was employed by Firestone, Wheeler had contacts at the track and would call the speedway daily to obtain updated practice reports on Guthrie. Smith and Wheeler also talked daily about the course of action to take regarding

World 600 ticket sales. Meanwhile, Max Muhleman, who had covered the inaugural World 600 for the *Charlotte News,* had returned to North Carolina from California and had his own marketing company. At the time, Charlotte Motor Speedway had only four full-time employees, so Wheeler enlisted his friend to help him.

Qualifying week for the World 600 arrived, and only about half of the Charlotte Motor Speedway grandstand had been sold. Ticket sales were lagging horribly. Wheeler knew Guthrie from her performance in the 24 Hours of Daytona, so he began calling her at Indianapolis, telling her there was another place she could race on Memorial Day weekend.

"I could tell she was a little reluctant to talk about it because I knew her whole goal was to make [the Indianapolis 500]," Wheeler said.

However, it wasn't in the cards that year for Guthrie to make the Indianapolis 500 grid. Her team was underfunded, and her car experienced numerous engine and mechanical problems during the month, preventing her from making a qualifying attempt. Guthrie's difficulties opened the door for Wheeler. The energetic, promotion-minded Wheeler jumped on the telephone and began pushing Guthrie to travel to North Carolina to race at Charlotte Motor Speedway. No woman had ever competed in stock car racing's longest race, and Wheeler saw this as just what he needed to boost ticket sales. Guthrie told Wheeler she would consider it if he could obtain the car A.J. Foyt had driven to the pole for the Daytona 500 that year even though Foyt's time had been disallowed due to NASCAR officials discovering evidence of nitrous oxide being used in the Hoss Ellington–owned Chevrolet to enhance the engine's performance.

Wheeler telephoned Foyt and told him he had two requests. One was to purchase the car he had raced at Daytona. The second was for him to put Guthrie, who had majored in physics at the University of Michigan, in his backup car and let her make some laps.

"I didn't want her to leave there without people knowing she could have made the race with a better car," Wheeler explained. "We finally made a deal after a lot of gnashing of teeth. I knew I would get pure hell over it from the drivers, but I had to do it."

Foyt always entered backup cars at Indy, and 1976 was no exception. His number one Coyote hadn't been qualified, so on the morning of the final round of time trials, the veteran competitor brought the car out of Gasoline Alley. After conferring with Foyt, Guthrie buckled into his car and posted a respectable 180.796-mile-per-hour lap. She had managed to get her problem-ridden mount up to only 173.611 miles per hour before it was withdrawn from time trials. The shake-down session was widely publicized, and then Foyt withdrew the car, saying he wanted to concentrate solely on winning his fourth Indianapolis 500 title and not a second car. Guthrie packed up and headed to North Carolina, with the media circus in tow.

Wheeler noted it was the first time he'd never had to call a press conference because the media was following Guthrie everywhere. Her every move was monitored, and now the motorsports spotlight had shifted from Indianapolis to Charlotte Motor Speedway.

Finding Guthrie a car owner was the next hurried order of business so that Wheeler could shift the heat away from Bruton Smith and himself. Women weren't allowed in the NASCAR garage at the time, and Wheeler hadn't counted on the upheaval Guthrie's arrival would cause. The competitors and NASCAR knew Smith and Wheeler had probably purchased the race car, but neither man would admit it. Enter thirty-two-year-old Lynda Ferreri, vice-president of First Union National Bank and one of the first women in management in Charlotte's banking industry. When Wheeler approached Ferreri about becoming Guthrie's car owner, she relished the idea.

Now Guthrie needed a crew chief. That duty went to Ralph Moody, a former driver who had become a renowned crew chief and co-owner of the famous Holman-Moody operation that was Ford Motor Company's racing arm in the 1960s.

Once Guthrie arrived in Charlotte, a press conference was held, which Wheeler described as "the biggest press conference I had ever been to except when [Mario] Andretti won the 500 and I was in charge of that one."

Wheeler remembered the ups-and-downs of the situation:

> *She said all the right things…we got tremendous publicity, but the garage area was brewing some scalding hot tea at the time. This was at a time when there still was not that much money in the garage area because all of the factories had pulled out. Firestone had pulled out. There was no tire money. Most guys were paying for their tires. They still had to buy all of their parts and pieces and there were no sponsors. RJR [R.J. Reynolds Tobacco Company] was in, but other than putting point money up and furnishing tracks with red and white paint, they weren't putting a whole lot of money in people's pockets. The factories had gone completely out of it. Even the sinister sliding of this and that [parts and deal money] wasn't there in any abundance. For anyone to have had a car furnished and a good one, that did not ride right, plus these guys didn't like the idea of racing against a woman.*

Ralph Moody served as Janet Guthrie's crew chief in 1976, but it was his message to Fred Lorenzen on his race car's dashboard reminding him to "Think" that caught everyone's attention years earlier. *CMS Archives.*

When Linda Ferreri arrived at the track, Bill Gazaway, who oversaw NASCAR's garage, wouldn't admit her even though she was listed as Guthrie's car owner. An angry Ferreri called Wheeler, who then contacted Gazaway and told him he'd better allow her in the garage.

"Well, he hemmed and hawed," Wheeler recalled. "I said, 'You want to do this easy or do you want to have to go to federal court and have to explain to a judge?'"

Gazaway immediately telephoned NASCAR president Bill France Jr., whom Wheeler expected to call him any minute. Instead, Gazaway called back and told Wheeler that Ferreri could come into the garage, but she'd better be wearing slacks.

When Guthrie couldn't get her car up to speed during practice, it was decided that she wouldn't participate in Wednesday's first round of qualifying. In those days, the starting grid was determined over a two-day period in an effort to gain pre-race publicity and boost ticket sales. With the large number of entries for the event, Guthrie stood a chance of not making the forty-car field with the practice speeds she had posted.

Even though cars usually weren't built for specific tracks in the 1970s, Daytona was the exception. The car Guthrie was driving had been constructed for the two-and-a-half-mile superspeedway, so it had a really slick body, which provided it with more speed down the straightaways, Wheeler explained. That's the reason it wasn't handling for Guthrie, Wheeler continued; she was getting more speed in the corners than the rest of the cars.

Junior Johnson possessed a reputation for producing good handling cars, so Wheeler asked for his assistance. Johnson and crew chief Herb Nab spent several hours with Guthrie, and her speed increased by 5 miles per hour. On Thursday, Guthrie qualified twenty-seventh with a lap of 152.797 miles per hour.

"It got a tremendous amount of publicity," Wheeler said. "The next day, Friday, we sold more tickets than we've ever sold in one day in the history of the speedway. We sold the last ticket late Friday. Bruton wanted to sell standing room only tickets, and that proved to be a big mistake. We had people standing in the aisles, making everyone else mad."

Guthrie finished fifteenth in the race, twenty-one laps behind winner David Pearson. Bruce Jacobi stood by in Guthrie's pit in case she needed a relief driver on that miserably hot Sunday afternoon, which saw many fans actually lying on the restroom floors in an attempt to get cool. The 4,100-pound stock cars didn't have power steering, and equipment designed for cooling the driver didn't exist. Jacobi's services weren't needed, however, and Guthrie earned the Curtis Turner Achievement Award for outstanding accomplishment in the race.

While the fans were glued to the on-track activities, they were unaware that Wheeler and his staff had found themselves in a water crisis.

"I made a bad mistake," Wheeler said. "It shows how when you're running a speedway, everything has an opposite reaction."

Just as any speedway general manager would, Wheeler was focused solely on monitoring ticket sales as race day approached. When then ticket manager Jean Bradley told him they were sold out, Wheeler inquired as to how many single tickets remained. She told him none—more single tickets had been sold than for any race previously held.

"That should have tipped me off, but it didn't," Wheeler said. "On race day I started seeing a lot of cabs come to the track. That had never happened before. You ask someone at the airport to take you to the racetrack in a cab, they look at you like they'd rather go to Nova Scotia, but it happened."

Then, halfway through the race, Wheeler's nightmare began. His brother, David, informed him the speedway was out of water. The five hundred thousand gallons of water that normally sufficed on race day didn't make it.

"I said that's impossible because the race had been sold out before," Wheeler recounted. "We'd sold only five hundred standing room only tickets, so that's not it. He said the storage tanks were sucking air."

Wheeler hadn't prepared for a tremendous increase in female fans attending the event due to Guthrie and the demand that they would place on the restroom facilities. Three hundred miles remained in the race, and the speedway was out of water.

Fortunately, operations manager Harvey Walters, who had worked with Richard Howard in that same position, formulated a plan. Wheeler recalled the idea with a chuckle:

> We got everybody we could find to call the list of volunteer fire departments that he had. We told each one of them we'd give them $500 if they would bring their tanker truck to the track and get there in thirty minutes. Twenty minutes later it looked like a nuclear leak at McGuire because all of these fire trucks are coming from 360 points with their sirens blasting.
>
> We always had a lot of pumps at the speedway because you never knew when a water line would break or the craziest things we had wouldn't work. We got all of the pumps together and took them and ran a hose up to the tank. We had two tanks on the ground and two high water tanks. We got it in there thanks to Harvey's backup plan, because I sure didn't have one.

That was a lesson Wheeler learned early in his speedway management career. From that day forward, the speedway staff always had a backup plan for every possible scenario. When the SAFER barriers came into use, Charlotte Motor Speedway workers practiced removing and replacing them so that the least amount of time would be needed on race day should one have to be replaced. (Developed at the Midwest Roadside Safety Facility at the University Nebraska–Lincoln, the Steel and Foam Energy Reduction [SAFER] Barrier, also referred to as a soft wall, was designed to absorb and reduce kinetic energy when a car hit the wall attached to the original concrete barrier. They were first installed at Indianapolis Motor Speedway in May 2002. NASCAR now requires all asphalt tracks hosting its top three series to have SAFER barriers.)

"We used to sit around and make up these really weird things, and then come up with a plan so if it did happen we would know how to react," Wheeler said. "It seemed like every time we thought up the worst thing that could happen and people would say, 'Oh that will never happen,' it would happen."

However, in all of the planning sessions for mass catastrophes, never did the possibility of one of the pedestrian bridges collapsing surface.

The unthinkable occurred immediately after the May 2000 Winston All-Star race. Dale Earnhardt Jr. had become the first-ever rookie to win the event, and his father joined him in Victory Lane to share his joy and excitement over the accomplishment. Thousands of race fans inside the track celebrated the popular victory, but for the hundreds who had already left the track and were headed to their cars, the joyous evening quickly turned into a horrifying experience. Fans walking across one of the pedestrian bridges that spanned Highway 29 suddenly felt the concrete shake, and the next thing they knew, the bridge collapsed beneath them.

It was 11:15 p.m., and the thirty-six-ton, eighty-foot section of concrete spanning the highway's southbound lanes had broken in half and collapsed onto the four-lane highway. The injured count totaled 107. The break in the concrete walkway resembled a drawbridge operating in reverse, dropping to a "V" in the center while each end remained atop its respective concrete pillar. Racing souvenirs and coolers carried by the fans littered the highway where their owners had plummeted to the pavement. A perimeter was quickly established, and medical personnel who were on duty or attending the event as fans rushed to aid the injured. The facility's newly constructed dirt track, which was close to the damaged pedestrian bridge, was turned into a landing zone for medical helicopters while about 50 of the 183 North Carolina Highway Patrol troopers assigned to the race rushed to the emergency. Also responding were Concord police, track security, Charlotte and Concord fire department personnel and at least three dozen ambulances from various counties. Where the sound of race cars once rumbled through the night air, there were now only sirens and the whirling of helicopter blades. A disaster alert was issued for all medical personnel in Cabarrus and Mecklenburg Counties, so they were prepared and waiting in emergency rooms at seven area hospitals when the injured began arriving. By 12:30 a.m., all of the injured had been removed from the twisted metal and concrete.

Wheeler noted it was the speedway's advance planning that had enabled the injured people to be transported to seven different hospitals within about an hour.

"Had we not had a plan for triage, that would never have happened," Wheeler said. "It was a horrible thing to go through, but it worked out well because everyone cooperated."

While the first responders treated the injured, then Speedway Club head Wanda Miller had her chefs begin preparing food for security personnel and EMTs working the scene.

"That taught us a lot about how things should be done," Miller commented.

No one was killed that night, but three were critically injured. One who was critical remained hospitalized for several weeks and was bedridden for most of the next year. He's now confined to a wheelchair and has lost a leg.

An investigation into the bridge collapse by the North Carolina Department of Transportation revealed rusted steel cables inside the concrete walkway.

Since Charlotte Motor Speedway opened in 1960, more than a half dozen drivers have lost their lives due to injuries sustained at the track, but in 1999, three spectators were killed and at least eight injured during an Indy Car race that more than a decade later Wheeler still referred to as a "horror story."

The tragedy occurred when a tire and suspension parts flew into the stands near the fourth turn after a three-car crash in the VisionAire 500.

"When I got over there, which was within minutes after it happened, there were three bodies, and other people were injured," Wheeler said solemnly. "I knew some big decisions had to be made—getting the injured out, proper treatment for them—and then the thought struck me about what to do about the race. I got back in the control tower, called Tony George [then head of the Indy Racing League] and I said, 'Look, Tony. I think we need to quit; just give everybody their money back and tell the drivers that's the way it is.' I think we made the right decision."

Throughout thirty-three years together, Smith and Wheeler made numerous right decisions even though they drew criticism for several of them, including lighting the speedway so racing at night could occur. Ultimately, however, that one decision changed the face of NASCAR forever.

CHAPTER FOUR

HOSTING THE ALL-STAR

S hort-track managers possess a unique, almost carnival-like style when they create promotions designed to generate excitement among race fans, and that skill is something Bruton Smith and Humpy Wheeler understand quite well. So when then series sponsor R.J. Reynolds Tobacco Company (RJR) announced in December 1984 that there would be an All-Star race in May 1985, Charlotte Motor Speedway immediately emerged as the front-runner to host it. It seemed like a natural decision because the one-and-a-half-mile speedway was the home track for the majority of the race teams. RJR agreed. In January 1985, RJR president Jerry Long made it official that on May 25, the inaugural Winston race would be held at Charlotte Motor Speedway. It was the first time such an event had been held for the Cup series since NASCAR president Bill France Sr. conducted All-Star races at Daytona International Speedway from 1961 to 1963.

Months of promotion preceded the race, which would be held the day before the Coca-Cola 600. The only drivers eligible for the event were the dozen who had won a Cup race in 1984. Series champion Terry Labonte started on the pole, with the rest of the starting lineup determined by the number of victories earned the previous year. Ties were broken by a driver's final position in the 1984 point standings.

Unfortunately, the race wasn't as exciting as the pre-race activities. Most of it was a strung-out, boring event. There were occasional bursts of side-by-side racing. However, what is remembered most about the event was the engine in Darrell Waltrip's Chevrolet Monte Carlo erupting in smoke just as he received the checkered flag.

Charlotte Motor Speedway owner Bruton Smith speaks during the press conference announcing the site for the inaugural All-Star race. RJR president Jerry Long is seated to the left. Drivers attending the event, from the left, are: Geoff Bodine, Harry Gant, Terry Labonte and Bill Elliott. *CMS Archives*.

"The boys told me, 'Don't run it long, just long enough to win the race,'" Waltrip said about his car's engine immediately after the event.

Harry Gant, who finished less than a second behind Waltrip, said he could smell the winner's engine when Waltrip passed him on lap sixty-nine of the seventy-lap event. In fact, the Taylorsville, North Carolina driver initially thought it was the engine in his Chevrolet that he smelled.

The inaugural All-Star race wasn't divided into segments, and the only special rule was the requirement that drivers make a mandatory pit stop between laps thirty and forty. A $10,000 bonus was awarded to the leader of lap twenty and lap fifty-five. Terry Labonte collected the first $10,000 while Gant took the second.

For winning the race, Waltrip received $200,000, the most ever paid for a stock car race.

"We're in the money. We're in the money," Waltrip kept singing as the media interviewed him after the event. "With about ten laps to go, I said to myself, 'Well, it looks like this is your year to finish second.' Then Junior [Johnson, car owner] called me on the radio and inspired me along. I won't tell you how."

Preparing for the inaugural All-Star weekend, from the left, are Benny Parsons, Michael Waltrip, Richard Petty and Dale Earnhardt. *CMS Archives*.

Geoff Bodine was the only driver who didn't finish the race. His engine expired in his Hendrick Motorsports Chevrolet on lap fourteen.

Entering the special event, Bill Elliott had been the favorite due to his dominating season on the superspeedways. However, the Dawsonville, Georgia driver had to settle for seventh.

"We had problems with the clutch slipping, and I had to hold the gear [shift] in place with one hand and drive with the other. That doesn't work too well at speeds like this. That short race seemed like a twenty-four-hour marathon," Elliott said.

When RJR conceived the All-Star race, it was to rotate to the Cup circuit's tracks. However, when it moved to Atlanta in 1986, it was a disaster in the attendance department. Scheduled for Mother's Day weekend, the attendance was extremely disappointing when compared to the number of spectators that had attended the inaugural event at Charlotte. An infield crowd was nonexistent, and the souvenir rigs experienced very little business.

It didn't take RJR long to decide to transport the All-Star race back north on I-85 to Charlotte Motor Speedway. What the 1986 race lacked in excitement, the 1987 event more than made up for. The fireworks that

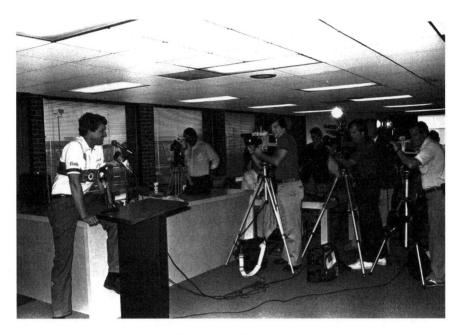

Bill Elliott was the favorite entering the inaugural All-Star race. This press conference was held in the speedway's first infield media center. *CMS Archives.*

erupted that day between Dale Earnhardt, Bill Elliott and Geoff Bodine are still discussed more than twenty years later.

A new format set the stage for the type of explosive ending that the race's promoters had been seeking. This time the All-Star race was divided into three segments of 75, 50 and 10 laps. The first two segments resembled the first two All-Star races with very little action. Bill Elliott led 71 of the first 75 laps and all 50 of those that composed the second segment. That meant by the time the twenty-car field reached the final segment, Elliott had led 121 of the 125 laps.

When the field lined up for the final segment, Elliott was first, Bodine second, Kyle Petty third and Earnhardt fourth. The top three drivers had been the only leaders in the first two segments; therefore, they were awarded the first three starting positions. Due to Earnhardt being the runner-up at the end of the second segment, he was awarded the fourth starting position for the final ten laps.

Now it was time for the ten-lap shootout, and one could sense there was about to be an on-track explosion that would send the event into the annals of legendary races. When the green flag waved, the cars sped toward the first turn and dove into the corner. Bodine had nudged slightly ahead of

Elliott, but entering the second turn, Elliott and Bodine touched. Then Bodine looped his Chevrolet. Elliott maintained Earnhardt instigated the incident when he hit him in the rear as they dove into turn one. None of the three cars was damaged, but Earnhardt had shot to the inside and into the lead when Bodine spun. Bodine had to pit for tires, but Elliott had held on to his mount during the incident and was in second when the field lined up for the restart.

The race's rules required that all ten laps in the final segment be run under green-flag conditions, and it was this segment that kept the screaming crowd on its feet. With seven laps remaining, Elliott was riding Earnhardt's bumper when the two cars bumped as they exited the fourth turn and raced through the dog-leg-shaped frontstretch. Earnhardt shot into the frontstretch's grassy apron, plowed through it for about 150 feet and then shot back onto the track to the roar of the crowd, still narrowly in the lead. Earnhardt's spectacular move became known as the "Pass in the Grass" even though it wasn't actually a pass.

The war was on between the two. One lap later as they raced through turn three, Elliott moved to the outside of Earnhardt. Clearly unhappy with what had happened earlier, Earnhardt squeezed Elliott to the wall. Earnhardt later maintained that he and Elliott never made contact, but Elliott disagreed, saying it was that move by Earnhardt that crumpled his car's left-rear fender against the tire. The damage cut the tire a lap later, and Elliott had to pit.

Terry Labonte had slithered into the lead during the Earnhardt-Elliott confrontation in the third and fourth turns, but by the time they reached the first turn on the next lap, Earnhardt had shot back into the top position. Earnhardt went on to finish 0.74 of a second ahead of Labonte to become the third different winner in the three-year-old event. An angry Elliott had to settle for fourteenth, and he was by no means finished with Earnhardt.

On the cool-down lap, Elliott blocked Earnhardt as they exited the first turn. On the backstretch, he swerved toward Earnhardt on the outside, forcing him to slam on the brakes so hard that smoke billowed from his car's tires. Elliott then cut off Earnhardt again at the pit road entrance and turned toward him one more time at the entrance to the garage area, forcing Earnhardt to move to the outside of pit road. The last maneuver occurred near Earnhardt's crew, which had been located just one pit space away from Elliott's team. Fists were shaken and words exchanged.

While the fans and media were focused on the Elliott-Earnhardt confrontation, another one occurred in the garage between Kyle Petty and

Kyle Petty gives young sons Adam (right) and Austin a ride in his race car in 1985. *CMS Archives*.

Rusty Wallace. Petty's father, Richard, separated the two before that situation got seriously out of hand. An exchange of sheet metal between those two drivers on the backstretch had left Wallace fifth and the younger Petty sixth in the rundown.

"I wasn't hot at Rusty, and I'm not mad at him," Kyle Petty said after he'd had time to cool down. "I just wasn't happy with what happened and that's what I went up to his car window to tell him after the race. I didn't like it because he turned left into me. The next thing I know he wants to fight."

No doubt some of the All-Star races have been more exciting than others. One of those was the 1989 event, when Rusty Wallace and Darrell Waltrip were pitted against each other in the closing laps. An incident in the fourth turn, when Wallace tagged leader Waltrip and sent him spinning through the frontstretch's grassy apron, quickly changed fans' attitudes toward Waltrip. The man who had always drawn thunderous boos from the crowd was now being cheered by the fans.

"He [Wallace] put me into the spin cycle, and when I came out, I was squeaky clean," chuckled Waltrip, who was sponsored by Tide at the time. He continued: "I had a fast car, and I fooled around there; and the first thing

I knew, Rusty and I were in a little bit of a race, but I didn't think he had anything for me. He overdrove the turn, got into me and spun me out. I went from the bad guy to the good guy in one swift spin right there."

More than twenty years after that altercation, Waltrip can now discuss it calmly and even laugh about it. That wasn't the case, however, that day. Wallace won, and while he was celebrating in Victory Lane, Waltrip angrily said he hoped Wallace choked on the $200,000. Their two crews scuffled and were still at odds the next week when they both showed up for lunch at the Sandwich Construction Company, a restaurant frequented by the racing community during that decade.

It wasn't until 1992, however, that Smith's and Wheeler's short-track-promoter backgrounds came into play with the All-Star race. The two men knew from their time promoting races on North Carolina's dirt tracks that racing under lights generated a special type of excitement and that the experience was something superspeedway racing desperately needed. Attendance figures at Bristol Motor Speedway in Tennessee soared after then owner Larry Carrier moved his August event to a night race in the late 1980s. RJR was considering moving the All-Star race to another track, something Smith and Wheeler didn't want to happen. That's when Wheeler met with RJR Sports Marketing Enterprises head T. Wayne Robertson and proposed to him that the All-Star race be turned into a night event. Robertson liked the idea. However, then NASCAR president Bill France Jr. didn't.

"He said, 'I don't believe the drivers will want to race,'" Bruton Smith recalled. "I said, 'Billy, that's what they've been doing their whole career, running Friday and Saturday nights under the lights.'"

France told Smith he wouldn't do it, but the determined Smith believed the radical idea of lighting a superspeedway would be fabulous. No NASCAR Cup race had ever been run at night, and no track longer than a mile in length had ever been lit. At issue was determining the amount of light needed for the television cameras while at the same time guaranteeing it didn't adversely affect the drivers' vision. Wheeler and Smith turned to Musco Lighting for the project.

"We got really lucky because one of the gentlemen from Musco had driven race cars," Smith said. "So when I talked with him, he understood what I was talking about."

Musco Lighting also made Smith a deal that would give anyone the confidence needed to take the gamble. If the lights didn't work, the company would remove them at no charge. Obviously, Musco never had to follow through on the agreement.

With Wheeler taking control of the monumental task and focusing on it daily, the $1.7 million project began to take shape after it was announced in late November 1991. Once it was completed, the new lighting system consisted of 1,200 fixtures; 56 poles, from 70 to 110 feet tall; 1,700 mirrors; 75 miles of wire; 160 tons of steel; 520 tons of concrete; and 11.5 tons of glass. Twenty-four semi-trailers were needed to transport the lighting equipment from Iowa, where Musco developed it, to North Carolina. Officials said the system used two million watts of power per hour—equivalent to the power required for all of the households in a town of five thousand people—and operated at a cost of approximately $140 per hour. Generators powered 8 percent of the lights as a safeguard in case there was a power outage. NASCAR monitored the installation.

On April 15, 1992, less than six months after it was announced, the system received its first test. That's when Smith pulled the switch to "officially" activate the lights before an estimated crowd of thirty-eight thousand that had shown up for the drivers' first night test. A shower of sparks, which had been purposely created for effect, rained down on Smith and slightly scorched the hair on top of his head. Those, however, were the only sparks of the evening. For the next three hours, fifteen NASCAR drivers practiced without incident under the lights on the superspeedway. All gave favorable reviews, and at least one predicted it would be the wave of the future for NASCAR's premier series.

Dale Earnhardt was the first to test the track under the lights, and Kyle Petty gave the project a five-star rating. Unofficial speeds during the three-hour test showed Geoff Bodine's Ford turning a 175.10-mile-per-hour lap (at that time, Charlotte Motor Speedway's one-lap qualifying record was 176.499 miles per hour). Harry Gant's Oldsmobile was second fastest at 173.021 miles per hour, while Bill Elliott's Ford was clocked at 170.562. Morgan Shepherd, also in a Ford, posted a 170.025-mile-per-hour lap, and Ernie Irvan's Chevrolet was timed at 170.347 miles per hour.

When the cars came close to the outside wall, they threw shadows on it. There were also shadows inside the cars, but the drivers didn't report any glare in their rearview mirrors. However, the competitors did request more lighting on pit road and in the garage. That night, the track had conventional lighting—poles surrounding the outside of the track and additional lights atop the suites—and Musco's new mirror-type lighting. The revolutionary lighting system developed by the Oskaloosa, Iowa company uses large mirrors aligned around the infield fence on the inside of the track. The system simulates daylight without glare, shadows or obtrusive light poles.

During the test, Mark Martin wore his smoke face shield on his helmet while Shepherd tested a pair of sunglasses with high-intensity yellow lenses. The sport glasses were developed by Oakley for bikers who race at night and marksmen who shoot in low light. Shepherd said he could see some dark spots on the track when he removed them.

Darrell Waltrip noted the lights flickering down the backstretch bothered him.

"They make my car light up inside when I go down through there and when you first see it, you want to look over and see what it is," Waltrip said that balmy night. "After a while, you kind of get used to it."

Waltrip and Davey Allison both reported that depth perception seemed to be the biggest issue. By the second night of practice, however, Allison apparently had solved the problem. He recorded a 175.598-mile-per-hour lap to walk off with $1,000, courtesy of Musco Lighting, for posting the quickest timed lap in the bonus money run. Of the drivers who participated in the second night of practice, Darrell Waltrip was the only other one who tried for the bonus money.

It was Petty, however, who truly possessed the crystal ball that evening.

"This could be the future of racing," Petty said that slightly overcast night. "You can make more of a package out of night racing, and it will sell better to TV."

Charlotte Motor Speedway billed the race as "One Hot Night," and the excitement triggered by the 1992 Winston All-Star race has yet to be surpassed twenty years later. Robin Pemberton was Kyle Petty's crew chief that night, and two decades later he equated the atmosphere at the event to a Rolling Stones concert. It was "electric" and "unbelievably cool," said Pemberton, who eventually became NASCAR's vice-president for competition.

Even twenty full-throttle stock cars couldn't drown out the roaring crowd that magical night. Each time the field lined up to receive the green flag, the thousands of camera flashes in the grandstands resembled twinkling stars in the night sky. A full moon added even more drama to the setting. It was a time in the sport when everyone liked to have fun—in and out of the race cars. Drivers could still look up in the stands during caution periods and see who was sitting in what seat, fistfights that were occurring between fans and girls wearing bikinis. The teams possessed good sponsors, but it wasn't as intensely corporate as today's environment. It was just hard racing week-in and week-out, and the 1992 Winston All-Star race exemplified that atmosphere.

Throughout the night the race had been building to a monumental climax. The final stage for the wild finish was set when Darrell Waltrip sailed through the frontstretch's grassy apron with seven laps remaining in the ten-lap shootout. For the restart, Petty lined up first with Dale Earnhardt beside him and Davey Allison at his rear. Earnhardt snatched the lead before two laps were completed, and Allison relegated Petty to third. Petty fought back and retook second on lap sixty-six of the seventy-lap event.

On the final lap, the three roared down the backstretch. Petty caught Earnhardt and dove to the inside. Earnhardt forced Petty low, but he was carrying so much momentum into the third turn that his Chevrolet broke loose and spun toward the outside wall. Petty had let off the throttle slightly to regain control of his car, allowing Allison, who never backed off, the few seconds he needed to catch Petty. Side-by-side they sped off turn four. There was a bump, then another and the shoving match continued to the checkered flag with the final tag sending Allison spinning in front of Petty's Pontiac and into the outside wall among a shower of sparks.

Allison was knocked unconscious, and the car's roof had to be cut away so he could be removed from the car. The young driver didn't even know he had won the race until team owner Robert Yates and crew chief Larry McReynolds visited him in the infield medical center. The accident left Allison with a bruised lung, bruised legs and a concussion. His Ford, nicknamed "007," was so battered it couldn't even appear in Charlotte Motor Speedway's Victory Lane for the fourth time in its last five starts at the track.

While medical personnel attended to Allison, Petty and Earnhardt drove their battered cars to the fuel pumps.

"Kyle gets out and our crew runs over there," Pemberton recalled. "'Big E' gets out, Will Lind, Chocolate [Myers], all those guys go running over there. Everybody thought there was going to be a brawl. Earnhardt grabbed Kyle by the neck and had that ol' Earnhardt smile."

There was no brawl, just two teams that had raced hard and enjoyed it. Richard Childress, Earnhardt's team owner, described that night as "a hell of a race."

Earnhardt smiled as he walked to his team's trailer after the event. The five-time champion always hated to lose, but the racing on the final lap was the type on which he thrived.

"I wish I could have won the race, but I ain't going to kick and scream about it," Earnhardt told reporters that night. "Kyle was trying to win and I was, too. I'm not going to be mad about it." Earnhardt continued to explain:

My car pushed a bit going into the second turn. I turned him [Petty] down where he was dragging and sparking. He went into the corner and tried to take what was his. That's all there was to it—good, hard racing. Kyle and I were just racing for it. He just took a little more than I wanted to give.

Of course, Petty's team was disappointed, and the loss even cost Pemberton a building lot on Lake Norman, something team owner Felix Sabates had promised the crew chief if the team won the All-Star race.

Many short-track operators were angry at Charlotte Motor Speedway for implementing night racing, but the major gamble taken by Smith and Wheeler changed NASCAR racing in its top three divisions forever. It made the races available for prime time television and often created a more pleasant environment for spectators who had endured sweltering heat at many events during the summer months.

Before the All-Star race was a decade old, Dale Earnhardt had taken possession of it by winning it three times. The only other driver to visit Victory Lane more than once in the special event was Davey Allison, but he had only managed to do it twice: in 1991 and 1992.

Earnhardt's third and final victory in the All-Star race came in 1993. This time, he shot past Mark Martin with just over a lap remaining in the ten-lap shootout to score the victory. The event, however, wasn't without controversy. Ernie Irvan had collected the $50,000 bonus that went to the winner of the first segment while Rick Mast picked up the same amount for taking the second. When they lined up for the final ten laps, Martin jumped past Mast and into the lead. It appeared the race belonged to Martin, but then, with just two laps remaining, Terry Labonte's Chevrolet spun and crashed between the third and fourth turns. His accident set the stage for the race's controversy.

When the race restarted with two laps remaining, Earnhardt jumped the restart, an act he admitted to after the race. NASCAR immediately waved the yellow flag, set the field again and then released it. Several competitors were irate that Earnhardt wasn't put at the rear of the field for jumping the restart. Irvan was one of them.

"The Winston is great, but let's not let somebody blatantly take a gun and steal the money. Let's race it out," said Irvan, who stormed into the team's hauler and slammed the door after the race. "If he [Earnhardt] wants to take somebody out for it, fine. That's not stealing the money. That's racing. To jump the start and give him another try at it is like giving a bank robber a second shot. It's like you didn't do it good enough the first time, try it again."

Earnhardt's response to the other competitors' complaints: "Well…I'm sorry."

"If you go back to the original rules for the Winston, NASCAR said anytime anyone jumped the restart, there would be a yellow flag," Earnhardt continued.

After the race, NASCAR explained that the yellow flag was thrown again after Earnhardt jumped the restart to ensure a fair one. Officials said that under normal circumstances a car on the outside, where Earnhardt was, in a double-file restart would have been on the lead lap and thus allowed to restart the race. However, because all the Winston restarts were double-file, that rule was no longer the case, and the restart belonged to the car on the inside, Mark Martin's Ford. (At this time, restarts for the point events had lead-lap cars on the outside and lapped cars on the inside.) Therefore, the officials, said, the yellow flag was waved to arrange another restart.

NASCAR also said it could have given the yellow flag to the field or the black one to Earnhardt, which meant he would have had to report to his pit. However, if NASCAR had displayed the black flag, it would have necessitated giving Earnhardt three laps before no longer scoring him. Due to the fact that there were only two laps remaining, he would have won by jumping the restart.

Even though controversy normally reigns in the All-Star race, there have been a few special moments. Such was the case in 1994, when Alan Kulwicki's team experienced a very emotional evening.

After Kulwicki, the 1992 series champion, died in an April 1, 1993 plane crash en route to Bristol, Geoff Bodine purchased Kulwicki's team. The car he drove to victory in the All-Star race's 1994 version had been ordered by Kulwicki after he lost a car in a crash during the March 1993 Atlanta race. The car was to have been used in the 1993 Winston All-Star event and the Coca-Cola 600. However, it wasn't completed at the race shop located behind the speedway until the fall of 1993. It made its debut in Charlotte Motor Speedway's 1993 fall race, the Mello Yello 500, with Bodine at the wheel.

After receiving the checkered flag at the 1994 All-Star race, the emotional Bodine turned the car around and made a victory lap around the track in the reverse direction, a move Kulwicki made famous and named the "Polish Victory Lap." Kulwicki had executed it when he won his first Cup race at Phoenix in 1988 and his championship in 1992 at Atlanta. Bodine later said it would be the only time he would do so to honor Kulwicki.

"I felt like Alan was in the car with me during those last few laps," Bodine said after the race. "A little over a year ago this team was Alan's. We did the lap in honor of him, and we dedicate this victory to him."

Controversy returned to the All-Star race in 1997, but this time it was in the car Jeff Gordon drove to victory, not in an on-track incident. Gordon acquired his second victory in the All-Star race using what had been called Hendrick Motorsports' chassis of the future. The chassis soon became known as T-Rex. A research-and-development chassis, it appeared to be a work of art on paper, but it hadn't been tested at Charlotte Motor Speedway.

"We really didn't know what it was going to do," Gordon said after the race when discussing the car that had only been tested at another Bruton Smith track, Texas Motor Speedway. "That's why we're not running it in a full-out points race because we needed to test it tonight."

Ray Evernham, Gordon's crew chief at the time, described it as a new-generation car but declined to specify how it was different. He said it was better structurally and safer. NASCAR, however, wasn't impressed and told Evernham never to bring the chassis to the track again. T-Rex became extinct after only one outing.

When the 2000 season arrived, Earnhardt fans were delighted that Dale Earnhardt Jr. had moved up to the Cup series to join his father. However, the electrifying performance he provided them in that year's All-Star race was more than they could have imagined. After surviving a brush with the wall, Earnhardt Jr. capitalized on what he would later call a "gutsy" decision to take on four fresh tires under caution with just eight laps remaining in the ten-lap shootout. When the race restarted, he ran down Dale Jarrett and passed the veteran to become the first rookie to ever win the All-Star race. His payday: $515,000.

The twenty-five-year-old Earnhardt had gained entrance into the event by claiming his first Cup victory earlier that year at Texas. However, during the second thirty-lap segment, it didn't appear he would be in contention for the victory when he had to make repeated pit stops to tighten loose lug nuts and then scraped the fourth-turn wall. The younger Earnhardt was chasing Rusty Wallace when, with ten laps remaining in the second segment, he clipped the wall, causing the car to become tight due to the damage it suffered.

"When we hit the wall, it bent the rear end or something and just made the car drive different," Earnhardt Jr. said after the race. "Before I hit the wall, the car was just as fast as it was at the finish."

Earnhardt Jr. managed to finish third in the second segment, the same position as in the first. Prior to the start of the final segment, he pitted for two tires. Then two laps into the final ten, Tony Stewart, Jeff Gordon, Joe Nemechek and Steve Park tangled in the first turn. That's when crew chief Tony Eury Sr. and Earnhardt Jr. made the "gutsy" decision to sacrifice track position for four fresh tires.

"I knew we had a top-five car when we put on two tires, but we had no chance to win the race," he said immediately after the event. "We didn't come here to run second or third. We came here to win and that was the only way we were going to do it."

When the race resumed, Earnhardt Jr. was sixth, and Dale Jarrett was leading. Once the green flag waved, Earnhardt Jr. headed for the front. With three laps remaining, he streaked past his father and Jerry Nadeau to claim second. By this time, Jarrett's Ford was spitting smoke out its rear. Earnhardt Jr. and Jarrett raced side-by-side down the backstretch before Earnhardt Jr. snatched the lead for good as they exited turn four.

"I didn't know when this race was mine," Earnhardt Jr. said. "I was leading the last lap of the race and didn't know if I was going to win it or not."

After changing into street clothes, Dale Earnhardt rushed to Victory Lane to congratulate his son.

"It's kind of funny for me to stand on the podium and hear people cheering, 'Earnhardt! Earnhardt! Earnhardt!' especially when I'm the only Earnhardt up there," Earnhardt Jr. said during his post-race interview. "That was kind of weird. I made sure the big Earnhardt hurried up and got there so I didn't feel so weird. He's the Earnhardt in the family and he's the reason people are cheering Earnhardt."

Twenty-seven years after the Winston All-Star race made its debut, Jimmie Johnson became the third driver to place three victories in the event on his racing resume. Johnson collected Hendrick Motorsports' seventh All-Star win just a week after providing the organization with its 200th Cup victory at Darlington. However, it was Johnson's All-Star victory celebration that provided one of the more entertaining moments in the race's history. After Rick Hendrick told his driver to come get him, Johnson convinced the sixty-two-year-old team owner to sit in the driver's window for a celebratory ride down the one-and-a-half-mile speedway's frontstretch.

"That was the dumbest thing I have ever done in racing," Hendrick said with a grin and a slight chuckle during the team's post-race interview with the media. "When I climbed in I got my foot hung in the dash, had his knee [Johnson's] pinned where he couldn't get to the clutch. I thought, 'I'm going to be like a busted watermelon out here.'"

Johnson kept his car in first gear but still had to keep it running at fifty to sixty miles per hour. Johnson said with a laugh after the race,

I had my arm around Rick's leg, trying to hang onto him. I could feel the wind pulling on him. He mentioned his foot was in the way. I couldn't get

to the clutch to push the clutch in to slow down. When you let off the gas in these Cup cars, the way the cam is, it will start loping or jerking real bad. I was afraid if that happened I'd throw him off the side of the car. When we stopped, you couldn't get your foot off and I had to take the steering wheel off.

Hendrick responded with a laugh, "I'm surprised I didn't get called to the [NASCAR] hauler."

"I was afraid somebody was going to throw a beer can at us and hit you in the head," Johnson replied with a laugh.

"I was surprised they were really nice," Hendrick came back. "Maybe they were all customers. They were all waving. I didn't get any fingers. Not one single finger and no beer cans."

No doubt, the All-Star race and Charlotte Motor Speedway were made for each other. They're both full of surprises, glitz and glamour and are never disappointing. Just the way Bruton Smith and Humpy Wheeler believed racing should be from the time the two men entered the sport.

CHAPTER FIVE

WE'LL HANDLE THINGS OUR WAY

One thing had become evident in the years since Bruton Smith had regained control of Charlotte Motor Speedway: things would be handled the way he and Humpy Wheeler wanted, and neither man cared if his actions created a hornet's nest. They weren't afraid to lock horns with anyone, whether it was NASCAR, R.J. Reynolds, a TV network or a competitor, and they were always available to talk with the media about it.

The two men hadn't even been in control of the speedway for a decade before they were embroiled in a marketing battle with series sponsor R.J. Reynolds. Ralph Seagraves oversaw RJR's special events department at the time, and he had made it quite clear that no other tobacco company was welcome in NASCAR's premier series. Wheeler, who admitted he and Seagraves argued constantly, believed that if RJR wasn't willing to contribute funds for special race promotions, then he was free to seek financial support elsewhere.

Wheeler turned to U.S. Tobacco Company, where friend Johnny Hayes oversaw the firm's motorsports program. With company head Lou Bantle giving a nod of approval, the Skoal Hard Charger Award for the 1981 World 600 was born. Under the program's format, money would be paid to the driver leading specific laps. Beginning with lap twenty, the lap leader award would be paid every twenty laps until the race concluded. Every time the lead-lap cars were on a money-paying lap, fireworks were launched behind the track's backstretch in an effort to create excitement. Wheeler believed the bonus program would cause the drivers to battle for the lead instead of riding around the track until one hundred laps remained.

"We did it with great fanfare. That's when it all hit the fan," Wheeler recounted. "NASCAR went completely berserk after RJR went berserk. Jerry Long was president of RJR at the time, and I knew he'd been talking to Billy France. Billy was all over me."

Seagraves was irate and told Charlotte Motor Speedway that RJR wouldn't offer any support for its upcoming World 600. Speedway executives responded that that didn't matter because the track had its own marketing department. Seagraves's reaction was to withdraw all of RJR's Sports Marketing Enterprises team from Charlotte Motor Speedway and not participate in the Memorial Day weekend classic. It was the only time in the three decades that the Winston-Salem, North Carolina–based company sponsored the series that RJR had no representation at the track. For the 1981 World 600, there was no signage, inflatables, Winston show car or Miss Winston. RJR employees were nonexistent. It was a promotion that nearly got Wheeler kicked out, and if it hadn't been for NASCAR founder Bill France Sr., the promotion definitely would have had an adverse effect on his career. Wheeler's savior was someone who telephoned France Sr. about the situation.

"He'd been through the factory wars in the '60s that cost him a ton of money, so he thought they [RJR] were confronting NASCAR, not Charlotte [Motor Speedway]," Wheeler said.

Wheeler noted that France Sr.'s misunderstanding of the situation resulted in him commenting, "We're not going to let any big company push us around."

"That really ticked RJR off," Wheeler continued. "That got me off the hook, a little bit, but Junior Johnson got mad at me, as did Darrell [Waltrip] and some of the other drivers who were loyal to NASCAR and RJR. Of course, Junior and Ralph were best buddies."

Then NASCAR president Bill France Jr. attempted to resolve the adversarial situation by calling Smith and talking with him. Smith told him he couldn't do anything with Wheeler because the deal with U.S. Tobacco Company was done.

Years later, Wheeler said the speedway was being threatened with things that could happen if the deal for the lap-leader program wasn't canceled: "When stuff like that happens in racing you get undercurrent, and you never know what is going to happen, who's plotting what. So I'm sitting there thinking, 'Is NASCAR going to drop the sanction?' I'd better get Lou on the phone."

Bantle was in France at the time, but he'd already heard about the confrontations when Wheeler contacted him. Throughout World 600 weekend, Junior Johnson wouldn't speak to Wheeler. He would only acknowledge his presence with hard looks. France Jr. would simply look at Wheeler and shake his head in disbelief.

It was about the middle of the summer in 1981 when Junior Johnson finally telephoned Wheeler. The veteran team owner told Wheeler he wanted him to bring his wife and spend the day with him and his wife at the mountain cottage they owned near the Blue Ridge Parkway. Wheeler knew Johnson had something planned, and he suspected it involved Charlotte Motor Speedway's status with RJR. A few days later, Wheeler confirmed his suspicions. Ralph Seagraves and his wife were going to be at the log cabin, as was T. Wayne Robertson, who worked closely with Seagraves at RJR. Johnson transported everyone to the cabin and left Wheeler, Seagraves and Robertson to talk while the wives went shopping.

"We're sitting on the front porch, and I just had to do this," Wheeler said in describing that day. "I took out a can of Skoal, took a pinch and put in a dip between my cheek and gum. I thought, if they're up here to make peace, they won't get too mad about it."

Robertson acknowledged that he saw Wheeler's actions, but the three men settled their differences. Wheeler said it was a good meeting and several events and promotions resulted from it, including the All-Star race, which made its debut four years after Wheeler's confrontation with RJR.

"It was traumatic going through it," Wheeler admitted, "but someone had to do it."

About the time Wheeler was having his major run-in with RJR, the speedway acquired a fledgling radio network known as Performance Racing Network (PRN), which had been formed in Bristol, Tennessee. At the time, Motor Racing Network (MRN), which was owned by International Speedway Corporation (ISC), broadcast the majority of the races. Hank Schoolfield had formed Universal Racing Network (URN) to broadcast NASCAR Grand National (Sprint Cup) races in the 1960s, and it remained in business until the early 1980s when it lost its final track to MRN.

Until Smith began building his racetrack empire in the 1990s, the only races broadcast by PRN in the 1980s were those at Charlotte Motor Speedway. A variety of people anchored the network in its early years, including Ken Squier, veteran broadcaster and radio personality Bill Connell, ESPN's Larry Nuber and WSOC-TV sportscaster Harold Johnson. Former NASCAR drivers Buddy Baker and Benny Parsons were also used as analysts on the broadcasts.

Fast Talk with Benny Parsons was one of the most popular radio shows ever created by the Performance Racing Network (PRN). Parsons is shown with wife Terri at the 600 Children's Charities Ball. *CMS Archives*.

In the late 1980s, Smith decided it was time to develop the network he now owned to where it produced shows in addition to the race broadcasts. Doug Rice was hired in 1988 from WSTP/WRDX in Salisbury, North Carolina, where he was the program director, morning show host and sports play-by-play announcer, to replace Jay Howard as Performance Racing Network's affiliates director. Howard left to form his own company, JHE Productions. At that time, PRN was so small that Rice's office was a closet in the Goodyear building, which housed the speedway's administration offices at the corner of Morehead Road and Highway 29. He moved into the Smith Tower when the speedway's offices were relocated to the seven-story building, but PRN didn't have its own studio until 1993 or '94. When PRN's *Fast Talk with Benny Parsons* made its debut in 1992, a seventh-floor conference room in the Smith Tower was used for the broadcast.

"We had a rolling case of broadcast gear that we would come in and set up on Mondays [in the conference room]," Rice said. "Nobody knew the difference."

Today, Rice is PRN's president and general manager. He also co-anchors all of the PRN race broadcasts with Mark Garrow at the tracks owned by Smith's company, Speedway Motorsports Incorporated. Headquartered at Charlotte Motor Speedway, PRN moved into its two-story stylish, contemporary, state-of-the-art studio in the ground level of the Smith Tower in 2009. It now has ten full-time employees and fifteen freelancers.

"We can do anything at the studio that any major market radio station or sports market network can do in the studio radio world," Rice said.

In addition to the race broadcasts, PRN produces three other shows to keep listeners up-to-date on issues and events in racing: *Fast Talk*, *Garage Pass* and the *O'Reilly Auto Parts Pit Reporters*. Mark Garrow's daily radio show, *zMAX Racing Country* and the *Wine Crush* also come through PRN.

"We also record audio for TV and radio all the time," Rice mentioned. "I would dare to say that every major driver in NASCAR has at some point used our studio to record audio [for a sponsor]."

Rice noted that PRN had grown from a network that was producing two races annually in the 1980s to one that now carries a third of the NASCAR races with a crew committed to excellence.

"I'm proud where the network has grown over time," continued Rice, who attended races at Charlotte Motor Speedway as a fan many years before he was employed by Speedway Motorsports. Rice continued:

Charlotte Motor Speedway has never held a dry, run-of-the-mill press conference. They always have a showmanship twist and visual for TV. In the mid-1980s, Alan Kulwicki won a lawn tractor race held at a Charlotte hotel. *CMS Archives*.

I'm grateful every day for the support Bruton has given us. Even though we do races all over the country there is still something very special going into the broadcast booth on a Sunday at Charlotte Motor Speedway. It's special because you know you're broadcasting from the absolute epicenter of NASCAR. Charlotte Motor Speedway has a tremendous history. I care a lot about the speedway.

The determination by Smith and Wheeler to handle everything their way, from special events to marketing and publicity, didn't always sit well with some people, but it always generated plenty of attention and focused the media on the track.

Such was the case after the 1987 Winston All-Star race. In that event, the altercation between Bill Elliott, Geoff Bodine and Dale Earnhardt resulted in damaged race cars and Earnhardt's wild maneuver through the frontstretch's grassy apron that became known as the "Pass in the Grass." The following year, in an effort to gain publicity for the upcoming All-Star race, then public relations head Tom Cotter sent a package containing a crumbled Coors beer can and an empty Levi Garrett package (representing Elliott's and Bodine's sponsors), as well as a bill addressed to Earnhardt for grass repair, to the media. The competitors weren't happy.

Humpy Wheeler also angered Cale Yarborough and Darrell Waltrip not long after he assumed the speedway's general manager helm. It actually began Labor Day weekend at Darlington Raceway during the 1977 Southern 500. The two men were eliminated in a four-car crash on lap 227. The accident was triggered when Waltrip hit the rear of D.K. Ulrich's car and sent him into Yarborough. Terry Bivins also was collected. When Ulrich cornered Yarborough and wanted to know why the South Carolina native hit him, Yarborough said he didn't, that Jaws had run into him. When Ulrich asked, "Who?" Yarborough retorted, "Jaws, Jaws Waltrip hit you."

It was the summer that the movie *Jaws* had been a box office smash, and Wheeler seized on Yarborough's remark as a great opportunity to gain publicity for the track's October race.

"That's just what a promoter wants to happen just before his race, and Darrell didn't appreciate that a bit, as you know," Wheeler said with a chuckle. "I decided I would make them both mad."

Wheeler telephoned a fishing captain in Shallotte, North Carolina, who was a friend to the track's then public relations head Joe Whitlock, on Monday before Wednesday's qualifying session. He was asked to catch the biggest shark he could find and bring it to Charlotte. The fisherman honored

Wheeler's request, caught him an eight-hundred-pound tiger shark, packed it in ice and headed to Charlotte Motor Speedway.

Wheeler recalled the event:

> *I told him when he got here I wanted him to call me but not to come into the speedway. I had a wrecker driver meet us where the motor home lot is now. We picked that shark up on a hook, and I told him I wanted him to take him over to the qualifying board where the guys all stood* [to watch the qualifying times]. *I told him to park it there, lock it and—I didn't care who told him to move it—to leave it there.*

At the time, Yarborough was sponsored by Holly Farms, and a chicken had been placed in the shark's mouth to make it appear the shark was eating the chicken.

Wheeler said, chuckling again,

> *the first call I got was from Darrell, and he was mad as a hornet. He said, "I know you did this. Get that thing out of there." It wasn't five minutes later I heard from Cale. "Why don't you leave well enough alone?" I acted like I didn't know how it got there. They knew who put it there.*
>
> *Then somebody called from NASCAR and wanted me to move it. I played dumb then. Finally, after it had been there for about three hours* [Bill] *Gazaway* [with NASCAR] *called me up and said, "I know you've had fun with this thing, but you really need to move it because it is really beginning to smell." By that time, everybody had seen it so we moved it. It was about a month before either one of those drivers would even speak to me.*

A much more serious confrontation occurred at the 2001 fall race, when Wheeler went toe-to-toe with NBC Sports/Turner Sports over the October 7 broadcast of the UAW-GM Quality 500. The issue occurred during the decade that Charlotte Motor Speedway was known as Lowe's Motor Speedway because naming rights to the facility had been sold to Lowe's, the home improvement warehouse based in North Carolina. On the Tuesday before the race, Wheeler discovered the network didn't intend to call the track Lowe's Motor Speedway because Lowe's hadn't purchased any advertising time. Wheeler maintained that was contrary to the television contract NASCAR had negotiated that began in 2001. Prior to then, each track had handled its own TV contract. A NASCAR executive confirmed the contract the sanctioning body had signed required the network to call the speedway by its official name if it referenced the speedway.

NBC/Turner had refused to mention the speedway by name in its qualifying and Busch Series (now Nationwide) telecasts. Instead, its on-air talent had said "NASCAR Winston Cup from Charlotte" and "NASCAR Busch Series from Charlotte." Lowe's executives had noticed the omission of the speedway's name during Thursday's qualifying session. Wheeler maintained that the contract required the race and track be called by its official name at least twice during the telecast.

"I was tired of getting pushed around by TV anyway, and I was mad at their attitude more than anything," admitted Wheeler, who was president of the track's owner, Speedway Motorsports Incorporated (SMI), as well as the speedway at that time. "I think they thought we were swamp people anyway."

The issue was eventually resolved the evening before the Cup race, but not until it became quite heated and NBC Sports president Ken Schander had to leave his son's soccer game in New Hampshire and fly to Charlotte to meet with Wheeler.

At one point, Wheeler sent armed guards and two trucks to evict the NBC/TNT trucks from track property. The satellite trucks were never removed from the property, but the security guards and tow trucks did remain in the TV compound back of the track's frontstretch for most of Saturday. During the height of the confrontation, off-duty Cabarrus County sheriff's deputies hired by NBC/Turner for security reportedly wouldn't allow track security personnel in the TV compound. Concord police officers then told the TV security people the compound was their jurisdiction, not the off-duty deputies'. That part of the speedway was inside the Concord city limits.

When the confrontation occurred, the Charlotte track was the only one at that time that had sold its naming rights. FOX had used the facility's proper name during its telecast of the Coca-Cola 600 in May of that year, reportedly due to a $5 million payment. Lowe's had spent an estimated $35 million in advertising with NBC during the past year, but none of that was with NBC/Turner's NASCAR coverage.

Terms of the settlement weren't disclosed, but the race telecast was shifted to TNT when NBC broke away from the pre-race show to cover problems in Afghanistan. The broadcasters did refer to the track by its corporate name during the telecast.

During the pre-race drivers' meeting, then NASCAR president Bill France Jr. apologized to NBC.

Wheeler noted:

> *Bill France and I argued for about thirty years on a variety of subjects. We really liked each other, but we argued all the time. I just thought he wasn't doing certain things, and he thought I was going overboard on many things.*
>
> *That afternoon of the NBC thing he said to Bruton, "Why don't you just tell Humpy to stay home tomorrow, and you and I will run it." Bruton wasn't biting on that. I get out there the next day, and everywhere France is going to be there is a policeman. The NASCAR control tower had a policeman outside the door, an extra one in the garage. They were there to keep me from going anywhere. I went anyway because I knew all those guys.*

Since Wheeler retired after the 2008 Coca-Cola 600 and Marcus Smith, one of Bruton's sons, assumed the position of president for SMI and the speedway, the confrontational issues have pretty much been confined to Bruton Smith and local government leaders over tax issues related to his decision to keep the speedway in Cabarrus County. Smith threatened to move the track out of Cabarrus County when he got into a dispute with city and county officials about the dragway he wanted to construct. The issues were resolved and the SMI chairman built zMAX Dragway, now known as the "Bellagio of Dragstrips," near the dirt track located across Highway 29 from Charlotte Motor Speedway.

Bruton Smith also said during a February 2013 interview with WBT-AM morning talk show host Keith Larson that he would be willing to purchase the NFL Carolina Panthers and upgrade Bank of America Stadium without using funds from state and city taxpayers if Panthers owner Jerry Richardson wanted to sell the team.

Bruton Smith may be in his eighties, but when it comes to SMI and the speedway empire he has built, things are still done his way.

CHAPTER SIX

HELLO, HOLLYWOOD

From Elvis Presley's 1960s movie *Speedway* to John Lassiter's 2006 computer-animated, comedy-adventure sports film *Cars*, Charlotte Motor Speedway has always attracted glamorous stars, Hollywood producers, world-class athletes and the politically connected. It afforded the opportunity to enjoy a motorsports environment filled with glitz and pageantry.

Politicians, including presidential and gubernatorial candidates, have also been regulars at the track. Mark Thatcher visited Charlotte Motor Speedway while his mother, Margaret, was serving as Britain's prime minister. During the last decade, North Carolina's governors have attended events and press conferences at the speedway. However, former governor Mike Easley is the only elected official possessing the distinction of having wrecked a race car at the track. Easley was testing his talents in a Hendrick Motorsports Chevrolet one day when he lost control of the car and hit the wall. Easley wasn't injured, but his successor, Governor Beverly Perdue, opted for a ride-along.

Even though it's not unusual to now see celebrities at various racetracks, Charlotte Motor Speedway executives realized the value of having them attend an event early in the track's history.

It began in 1961 when Bruton Smith and Curtis Turner convinced English model and actress June Wilkinson to attend the second annual World 600. Wilkinson was known for her appearances in *Playboy* magazine and films of the 1960s. She was considered one of the world's most photographed women in the late 1950s and '60s.

June Wilkinson attended the 1961 World 600. For this photo, she posed on the hood of Curtis Turner's Wood Brothers Ford. *CMS Archives.*

In the 1970s, Elizabeth Taylor and Zsa Zsa Gabor graced the speedway's Victory Lane. Taylor served as grand marshal for the World 600 in 1975, and Gabor followed in 1976. When Taylor appeared at the track, she was living in Virginia with then husband John Warner, who waved the green flag for the race held the day before the World 600. At the time Gabor traveled to Charlotte, she was the national goodwill ambassador for the Chicago-based Montgomery Ward Auto Club. In that decade, the Hollywood Foreign Press Association had voted her the most glamorous actress in the world five consecutive times and the best-liked American actress in France.

Bruce Jenner (right) talks with NASCAR team owner Bill Gardner. *CMS Archives.*

In 1980, Olympic decathlon winner Bruce Jenner traveled to Charlotte Motor Speedway. At the time, he co-hosted NBC's *Sunday Games*, a television show that covered such outlandish events as the Union Tug-of-War and the World Belly Flopping contest.

The early '80s also brought evangelists Jim and Tammy Faye Bakker to the track on a regular basis when their TV show the *PTL Club* was in its heyday.

Even the host of ABC's long-running show *American Bandstand*, Dick Clark, took time to be the National 500 grand marshal one year. An article in the race program touting Clark's position for the race quoted him as saying he had been a "race fan for years" and had seen many events on the West Coast.

"I've heard that Charlotte is one of the best racing facilities in the world, and I'm honored to be asked to come to the National 500 and be the Grand Marshal for the race," Clark, who at the time was hosting the TV game show *$50,000 Pyramid*, said in the race program article.

Two stars from the Emmy-winning television show *Hill Street Blues*, Bruce Weitz and Ed Marinario, showed up for the twenty-third annual World 600. Weitz played undercover vice cop Belker while Marinario portrayed officer Joe Coffey in the NBC crime drama. The two men served as race co-directors.

In October 1990, retired Lieutenant Colonel Oliver North and Randy Owen, the lead singer for the popular country group Alabama, participated in race-day activities at Charlotte Motor Speedway. North, whose role in the sale of arms to Iran during the Reagan administration caused much controversy, was the honorary race director for that year's Mello Yello 500. Owen, who had performed in Charlotte with Alabama two days before the Cup race, sang the national anthem during the pre-race activities.

Other celebrities who have visited Charlotte Motor Speedway include movie producer Hal Needham—a former NASCAR team owner and stuntman who was presented with an honorary Oscar for his service to the movie industry during the 2013 awards ceremony—actor and singer Jimmy Dean and Barbi Benton of *Playboy* fame. However, perhaps one of the favorite stories surrounding a Charlotte Motor Speedway grand marshal involved world heavyweight boxing champion Joe Frazier, who attended the 1978 October race, and included Jim and Tammy Faye Bakker.

Former *Charlotte Observer* motorsports writer Tom Higgins recounted the story for ThatsRacin.com in November 2011, just two days after Frazier's death. Humpy Wheeler told Higgins that Frazier was a natural for Charlotte Motor Speedway because he was from Frogmore, South Carolina, near Beaufort, and he was very famous and popular at the time, having defeated Muhammad Ali a few years earlier. He also wanted Frazier to sing the national anthem so Charlotte Motor Speedway would be the first track to have an African American perform the song. Wheeler had heard him sing "The Star-Spangled Banner" a few weeks earlier at the Ali–Leon Spinks fight in New Orleans, and it had been a fabulous performance.

There was only one problem in booking Frazier. When he retired from boxing he had formed a band, the Knockouts, and the fourteen-member group had to perform the night before the Charlotte race at a Reading, Pennsylvania nightclub. Wheeler told Frazier he would send a plane for them. The former boxer didn't like small planes, but Wheeler, who had been a Carolinas Golden Gloves champion as a teenager, convinced him everything would be all right.

On Frazier's arrival at the track on race morning, he asked Wheeler if he could take a shower. Wheeler had a large bathroom adjacent to his office, so he turned it over to Frazier. While Frazier showered, Bruton Smith's invited guests, Jim and Tammy Faye Bakker, arrived at Wheeler's office for their first race. Wheeler was talking with the couple when Frazier started calling for a towel and the speedway president had to head him off before he walked into the room.

Wheeler escorted Frazier into the drivers' meeting and later watched the race with him from the roof above the press box. Higgins quoted Frazier, who was watching his first race, as saying, "It's rough. It's tough out there. When you make a bad move in boxing, you sometimes get hit. Make a bad move out there and you ain't around to smell the roses."

Wheeler told Higgins that Frazier really "hit it off with the fans" and that he was "accessible and friendly," more popular than Elizabeth Taylor when she visited the speedway.

Despite the numerous celebrities who have attended Charlotte Motor Speedway through the years, it's the track's role in numerous movies that will always keep it a favorite in Hollywood and endeared to the fans.

Hollywood actually discovered Charlotte Motor Speedway quite early in the facility's existence. Portions of Elvis Presley's 1968 movie *Speedway* were filmed at the track, but Presley never set foot on the property. Pal Parker, who was the speedway's photographer at the time, took photos of various track sites the director requested and shipped them to Hollywood so the sets could be constructed. Parker said some of the scenes where the cars were on the track were filmed at Charlotte Motor Speedway, but NASCAR driver Neil "Soapy" Castles handled the majority of the driving.

The opening scene in *43: The Petty Story* was filmed at Charlotte in May 1972 and released two years later. Richard and Maurice Petty play themselves in the movie, while Darren McGavin portrays their father, Lee. Timmy Petty, Maurice's son, is also in the movie in addition to Dale Inman and Buddy Baker. The movie is also known as *Smash Up Alley*.

Born to Race was a movie that was made at the track and then disappeared. And it was probably a good thing that it did. Humpy Wheeler said when he saw the movie, in which he participated, his mouth was moving but the voice that was coming out on screen didn't belong to him.

The scene in *Talladega Nights: The Ballad of Ricky Bobby* when Will Ferrell's character Ricky Bobby is running down the track because he thinks he's on fire was filmed on the track's backstretch. Filming occurred during a race week, and each night after the day's activities had been completed, the movie crew took over the backstretch near the tunnel.

However, it would be safe to say that Charlotte Motor Speedway starred in the racing movies *Stroker Ace* and *Days of Thunder*.

Filmed in the early 1980s and released in 1983, *Stroker Ace* director Hal Needham involved as many people as possible from the racing community in the action comedy that starred Burt Reynolds, Loni Anderson, Ned Beatty, Jim Nabors, Parker Stevenson and Bubba Smith. Harry Gant drove Needham's Skoal Bandit at the time on NASCAR's Cup circuit and always was included in the veteran stuntman's movies. Members of the racing

Even the inaugural World 600 program cover had a unique flair to it.

In the 1960s, TV reporters actually had access to drivers during a pit stop. Here Chris Economaki interviews the Wood Brothers' driver while the Stuart, Virginia crew executes a pit stop. *CMS Archives*.

In the 1970s, multicolored awnings provided shade to those sitting in the top rows of the frontstretch grandstands. *CMS Archives.*

David Pearson (21) leads Darrell Waltrip (88) and Richard Petty (43) into the first turn during the 1970s. It was a decade dominated by Pearson and Petty, but Waltrip served as a notice that the sport's next generation was nipping at their bumpers. *Bob Dudley/CMS Archives.*

David Pearson and his potent Wood Brothers Mercury dominated time trials at Charlotte Motor Speedway in the 1970s. From October 1973 through October 1978, Pearson claimed eleven consecutive poles. *CMS Archives.*

Janet Guthrie became the first woman to compete in the World 600 in 1976 and finished fifteenth. Her NASCAR debut in stock car racing's longest race resulted in a sellout crowd for the speedway. *CMS Archives.*

Darrell Waltrip won the inaugural All-Star race in 1985, blowing the engine in his Budweiser-sponsored, Junior Johnson–owned Chevrolet just as he received the checkered flag. *CMS Archives*.

Rusty Wallace celebrates his October 1988 victory in the Oakwood Homes 500. His only other wins at the one-and-a-half-mile track came in the 1990 Coca-Cola 600 and the 1989 All-Star race. *CMS Archives*.

The lavish Speed Club offers fine dining and special events year round. *CMS Archives.*

When the All-Star race was held under the lights for the first time, it was indeed "One Hot Night," as billed by the speedway. Kyle Petty (42) and Davey Allison (28) banged sheet metal as they raced for the checkered flag. The last hit spun winner Allison into the outside wall. *CMS Archives.*

Alan Kulwicki leads the field through the dog-leg-shaped frontstretch during a segment of the 1992 All-Star race. Dueling side-by-side behind him are Ken Schrader (inside) and Darrell Waltrip. *CMS Archives*.

Davey Allison celebrates his 1991 victory in the All-Star race with wife Liz. Allison was the first driver to win the event two consecutive years. *CMS Archives*.

Harry Gant earned three poles but only one victory at Charlotte Motor Speedway in the early to mid-1980s. His lone win at CMS came in the 1982 National 500. *CMS Archives*.

Jeff Gordon is one of nine drivers whose first NASCAR Cup victory has come at Charlotte Motor Speedway. Gordon defeated Rusty Wallace for his win in the 1994 Coca-Cola 600. *CMS Archives*.

Dale Earnhardt claimed his second All-Star victory in 1990. Here he celebrates the win with (from the left) team owners Judy and Richard Childress, Miss Winston, his wife, Teresa, and crew chief Kirk Shelmerdine. *CMS Archives.*

Charlotte Motor Speedway has grown from humble beginnings into one of the world's top racing facilities. *CMS Archives.*

A jubilant Dale Earnhardt embraces his son in Victory Lane following Dale Earnhardt Jr.'s win in the 2000 All-Star race. Earnhardt Jr. was the first rookie to ever win the event. *CMS Archives.*

The media swarms Ryan Newman after his 2002 victory in the All-Star race. Newman won the event in his rookie season, making him the second driver to accomplish the feat. *CMS Archives*.

Mark Martin (left) talks with Sterling Marlin during driver introductions. Martin has had four wins at Charlotte Motor Speedway. Marlin visited Victory Lane only once in a points race before retiring. *CMS Archives*.

Twice Tony Stewart has driven in the Indianapolis 500 and the Coca-Cola 600, which are held on the same day. In 1999, he finished ninth in the Indy 500 and fourth at Charlotte. Two years later, he placed sixth at Indianapolis and third at Charlotte. *CMS Archives*.

Jimmie Johnson (48), Steve Park (1) and Tony Stewart battle for position. Note the retaining wall has Lowe's written on it. From 1999 to 2009, Lowe's purchased the naming rights to the track. The initial ten-year deal was for $35 million, and a one-year extension was added. The track's name reverted to Charlotte Motor Speedway in 2010. *CMS Archives.*

Charlotte Motor Speedway president Marcus Smith (left) and 2012 NASCAR Sprint Cup champion Brad Keselowski unveil the $1 million bonus Speedway Motorsports chairman Bruton Smith will pay to the driver who wins all three segments in the 2013 All-Star race. *John Davison Photo.*

Created by 600 Racing, Legends cars provide a racing opportunity to aspiring drivers. The cars are marketed internationally and race every Tuesday, June–August, at Charlotte Motor Speedway in the Summer Shootout Series. *John Davison Photo.*

When the world's largest HG TV was installed above Charlotte Motor Speedway's backstretch, race fans were guaranteed not to miss any action on the track. *John Davison Photo.*

Clint Bowyer had to walk into Victory Lane in October 2012 due to his Toyota running out of fuel after he received the checkered flag. However, that certainly didn't dampen Bowyer's celebration. *John Davison Photo.*

Movie director Hal Needham was a regular fixture in the garage in the 1980s, when he owned the team that fielded cars for Harry Gant. *Bill Nivens/CMS Archives*.

community who appeared in the film included Betty Jane France, Cale Yarborough, D.K. Ulrich, Kyle Petty, Ricky Rudd, Dale Earnhardt, Neil Bonnett, Richard Petty, Terry Labonte, Benny Parsons, Tim Richmond, Chris Economaki, David Hobbs, Alexis Leras, Johnny Hayes, Johnny Bruce and Ken Squier. The movie's final scene was filmed in Charlotte Motor Speedway's Victory Lane and included speedway employee Darlene Dixon as one of the Skoal Bandettes.

The theme song was performed by Charlie Daniels, and the world premiere was held at Ovens Auditorium in Charlotte, North Carolina. All of the movie's stars, except Reynolds and Anderson, attended the premiere and the lavish reception on the auditorium's lawn afterward.

In an interview with a United Press International reporter during the movie's filming, Burt Reynolds said he was surprised at the greeting he received from the NASCAR drivers.

"They seemed genuinely interested in the picture business," Reynolds told the reporter. "I was taken by [Cale] Yarborough, [Richard] Petty and Benny Parsons. They're so warm."

At the time the movie was filmed, Reynolds was riding a wave of popularity due to his movie *Smokey and the Bandit* and co-owned the

NASCAR Cup team that fielded cars for Harry Gant with longtime friend Hal Needham.

Reynolds noted that auto racing first caught his attention when he was a high school student in Florida and he followed a driver who competed at a West Palm Beach, Florida track. He also watched the sport on television, but it was Needham who triggered his intense interest.

When asked what impressed him the most about the sport, Reynolds replied it was the drivers' camaraderie.

"I find them to be warm and with a great sense of humor and fun," Reynolds said. "It's obvious they are doing something they want to do and are making a living. Even those who are struggling enjoy it."

Reynolds also couldn't believe the two-way radio conversations between drivers and their crew chiefs during an event. He noted that he had listened to Gant and crew chief Travis Carter discuss a problem on the car during the Southern 500 and couldn't believe the calm in their voices.

Tom Cruise's movie *Days of Thunder*, which was released in 1990, also had a premiere in Charlotte, but it wasn't as lavish as the one for *Stroker Ace* or for the movie *Cars* many years later. Based on the relationship between veteran crew chief Harry Hyde and his flamboyant driver Tim Richmond, producers Don Simpson and Jerry Bruckheimer and director Tony Scott took actual events that had occurred at various times in the racing community and interwove them into a screenplay.

A press release distributed by the speedway's communications department said figures released by the Charlotte Convention and Visitors Bureau showed the thirteen days of filming at the track for the Paramount Pictures movie contributed nearly $250,000 to the Charlotte-area economy. The estimated contribution was $232,343, a $17,872.53 a day average. That figure included hotel rooms, incidentals, restaurant expenditures, catering, local transportation and miscellaneous expenditures. A staff of nearly 150 people spent ten days in December and three in January working on the motion picture in the Charlotte area.

It was the world premiere of *Cars*, however, that had everyone talking inside and outside the racing community. Held at the track, it was attended by most of the drivers competing in NASCAR's Sprint Cup Series. In this movie, Humpy Wheeler was the voice for the head of Dinoco, while other cars in the Pixar movie had the voices of Richard and Lynda Petty, Dale Earnhardt Jr., Mario Andretti, Paul Newman, Michael Schumacher and Jay Leno.

Wheeler said meeting John Lasseter, who developed the story and directed and co-produced the movie, was one of the special memories he has from his three decades at Charlotte Motor Speedway. He invited Lasseter to the North Carolina track and told him he needed to spend two nights in a motor home in the infield near a section known as Red Neck Hill.

"That's where the character Mater came from," Wheeler said. "There was a guy there who was actually named Mater. He was a construction superintendent who had worked on jobs at the speedway. Mater is the one who called John [Lasseter] one day and said, 'John, I got an idea. You're going to make this truck Mater, so why don't you make it Tow-Mater?'"

Wheeler said he also suggested to Lasseter that he put a Hudson in the movie. Wheeler continued:

> *When I went out there and saw what they were doing and saw the first pastel drawings of some of the characters it blew my mind. It was really, really neat. I thought this is going to do more for racing than has ever been done.*
>
> *He asked me what he should do about NASCAR. I said nothing. It's not about NASCAR. I called Brian* [France, who became NASCAR's chairman and CEO in October 2003] *and told him not to sweat it, to tell everybody to back off. This is going into every country in the world in forty languages. I'll give Brian credit. He saw the big picture and backed off.*

Having the movie's premiere at Charlotte Motor Speedway was no easy task, especially since it was done during the week of the Coca-Cola 600. Half of the infield had to be closed off for the event, and then everything had to be cleared within twelve hours after the premiere festivities had concluded. In preparation for the premiere, Projects of Interest owner Tom McClain, who served as the event's technical director, designed four screen structures for 120- by 50-foot picture sheets and a central stage for a live pre-show. He then supervised the install and created the load-in and load-out schedules.

McClain began with developing 3D CAD drawings for approval by his client and NASCAR. The screen array was 1,000 feet wide in front of the second-turn grandstand. Driver's-eye views also were created to show the competitors what to expect during practice, which occurred during the load-in. StageCo provided thirteen trucks loaded with steel and scaffold for the screens and central stage. Each screen structure was 75 by 120 feet.

Portable lighting towers created for Super Bowl shows were used for the pre-show concert that featured Rascal Flatts, thus aiding in the twelve-hour departure time. Safety also had to be considered because each screen measured six thousand square feet. A twelve-person crew was assigned to each screen in the event high winds should strike the speedway.

The day of the premiere kicked off with the popular *Live! With Regis and Kelly* morning show being broadcast from the track's second turn with the audience seated on the apron. An afternoon thunderstorm caused a delay in the program's beginning, but the 160 people on the project still managed to get everything cleared from the speedway by 1:00 p.m. the following day, just an hour past deadline.

Wheeler believes the movie will have a long-term benefit for the sport because the children who watched it when it was released will one day be adults, and the movie will be embedded in their minds.

"It will be like *Snow White*. It will keep being released and more kids will watch it," Wheeler explained.

And with Charlotte Motor Speedway continuously in the movies and on television, more people will want to experience it.

CHAPTER SEVEN

FIRST-TIME MEMORIES

Charlotte Motor Speedway has been not only a leader in the motorsports industry but also a track that has provided drivers with a special time in their career—that moment when they etch their names in the record books as winners.

Ryan Newman and Aric Almirola earned the first poles of their Cup careers at the one-and-a-half-mile track, both in preparation for the Coca-Cola 600. Newman's accomplishment came in May 2001, while Almirola claimed the number one starting position for the 2012 event.

Butch Mock and Bob Rahilly, co-owners of Rahmoc Enterprises, enjoyed their first Cup victory as team owners in the May 1983 version of the six-hundred-mile race, when Neil Bonnett defeated Richard Petty by less than a second.

For Adam Petty, it was the site of the only victory in the personable young man's brief career. No one who was there that night will ever forget that famous Petty smile flashed in Victory Lane by Adam, his father Kyle and grandfather Richard after the September 1998 ARCA race.

In NASCAR Sprint Cup racing, nine drivers, four of whom have gone on to earn series championships, can look to Charlotte Motor Speedway as the site of their first career victory. David Pearson was the first to gain the distinction that continued with Buddy Baker, Charlie Glotzbach, Jeff Gordon, Bobby Labonte, Matt Kenseth, Jamie McMurray, Casey Mears and David Reutimann.

"It's hard to explain that feeling between being just a driver and then being a winner on a big stage," Baker once said. "You don't know whether to show your emotions or try to hold them back and look like everybody else that ever won a big race. But that first one, if you don't let it out, I think you would explode. Nothing will ever compare to your first major win."

When twenty-six-year-old David Pearson pulled off a stunning upset in the 1961 World 600, the Spartanburg, South Carolina driver couldn't even name the crewmen on his winning team. That's because Pearson was selected to drive the Ray Fox–owned Pontiac the week of the race. In fact, when Fox picked Pearson, the 1960 series rookie of the year had just about

David Pearson was just twenty-six years old when he collected his first NASCAR Cup victory in the 1961 World 600. He was selected for the ride the week of the race. *CMS Archives*.

given up hope of being able to compete on the circuit. He already had been forced to park his own Chevrolet due to financial reasons.

Pearson received the opportunity to pilot Fox's car when Darel Dieringer wasn't available. Fox once said he didn't know everyone who talked with him about putting Pearson in his car, but he knew that Joe Littlejohn, Cotton Owens, John Bruner Sr. and Norris Friel all believed the young driver would do a good job.

It was the race's finish, however, that provided a glimpse into the stellar stock car racing career that awaited Pearson. Pearson led the final 129 laps in the grueling event but crossed the finish line in a shower of sparks due to his car blowing a tire with 2 laps remaining. Pearson possessed a 4-lap advantage at the time and refused to relinquish it, pushing his mount to the checkered flag on three wheels. Fireball Roberts finished second, 2 laps behind the determined Pearson. Rounding out the top five, respectively, were Rex White, Ned Jarrett and Jim Paschal.

Buddy Baker was next on Charlotte Motor Speedway's agenda of first-time winners. It was October 1967, and by this time in the season, most felt Richard Petty was unstoppable. He'd won ten consecutive races entering the National 500 and had already sewn up his second series championship even though two races remained in the season. Like Pearson, Baker drove a Ray Fox–prepared car, but this time it was a Dodge. The victory also didn't come early in Baker's career. He actually made 215 starts before getting to visit Victory Lane, and he didn't mind letting everyone see his tears of joy as he celebrated.

Baker led four times for 160 laps, including the final 78 circuits, to finish 1 lap ahead of Bobby Isaac in an event that experienced a high attrition rate. Only fourteen of the forty-four cars that started the race finished, but fans were still treated to an event that had twenty-two lead changes among seven drivers. Dick Hutcherson finished third, 2 laps off the pace, while Charlie Glotzbach was fourth, 5 laps back. G.C. Spencer took fifth, 6 laps in arrears.

One year later, Glotzbach became the third driver in Charlotte Motor Speedway's first decade to visit Victory Lane for the first time in NASCAR's top series. His win also ended an eight-year drought on NASCAR's superspeedways for car owner Cotton Owens, whose only other victory had come at Atlanta in 1960 with Bobby Johns driving.

Glotzbach, nicknamed "Chargin' Charlie," had earned the pole for the race eleven days earlier with a 156.060-miles-per-hour lap. The race had been rain delayed due to Hurricane Gladys sweeping up the East Coast, and it was the remnants of four days of heavy rain that shifted the race in Glotzbach's favor. Paul Goldsmith, who was leading with thirty-five laps remaining, was making his final pit stop when he swerved his Dodge to miss a crewman working on another car. His car slid into the muddy apron separating pit road from the frontstretch. It took several seconds to free the stuck car. Goldsmith ended the race in second, seven seconds behind Glotzbach, an Edwardsville, Indiana native. Rounding out the top five, respectively, were David Pearson, Bobby Allison and Cale Yarborough.

Glotzbach had made his first NASCAR start in 1960, but he didn't have a full season on the circuit until 1968. Therefore, his first victory came in only his thirty-sixth start.

"Our first win couldn't have come at a better time," Glotzbach said that day. "The cupboard was getting pretty bare after all the weird things that have happened to us. I had begun to think that bad luck was going to badger us from now on, but this wipes out all the bad breaks by a longshot."

It would be another twenty-six years before the spotlight would shine on a Cup series first-time winner at Charlotte Motor Speedway, and just as in 1968, it would be a driver who had spent his teenage years in Indiana.

Jeff Gordon was in only his second full-time season in the Cup series when crew chief Ray Evernham decided to order only a two-tire change on the final stop. It was generally accepted that a four-tire change was the way to go, and that was the path taken by veteran Rusty Wallace, who was battling the twenty-two-year-old Gordon for the victory.

It was only the second time the circuit's longest race had ever started during the day and ended at night, still a new environment that would provide the competitors with a constantly changing track surface that's always been temperature sensitive.

Jeff Gordon was driving a car that had been rebuilt after a wreck the previous weekend in the Winston Select All-Star race. In the first round of qualifying, his performance was terrible as he finished fourth from last. However, when a rain delay provided Gordon with a second chance, he claimed the pole with a sizzling 181.439 miles per hour.

When the race began, however, it was Rusty Wallace who owned the dominant car. He first appeared at the front on lap 164 and then dominated the remainder of the race, leading the most laps. It appeared Wallace was headed for a Coca-Cola 600 victory, but then with fewer than 100 laps remaining the race took a drastic change. There was no caution flag during the final 77 laps, and one by one the lead-lap drivers pitted for a final fuel stop.

After all of the other lead-lap cars had pitted, crew chief Ray Evernham made the call that caught everyone off guard. Evernham called for a two-tire change while the other drivers had received four. Naturally, a two-tire stop would be quicker, but the question on everyone's minds was whether Gordon would be able to hold off his fellow competitors who were piloting cars with four fresh tires.

Gordon received right-side tires and returned to the track in second, behind Ricky Rudd, who was attempting to claim the victory via fuel mileage. However, with nine laps remaining Rudd had to stop for fuel, and Gordon inherited the lead. Wallace attempted to catch the young driver but fell short by 3.91 seconds.

The magnitude of Gordon's accomplishment was overwhelming for him. He fought off tears as he took the checkered flag but then collapsed in his fiancée's arms in Victory Lane and cried.

Bobby Labonte would follow Gordon a year later and snare his first career Cup victory in the May 1995 Coca-Cola 600. Labonte was in his inaugural season with Joe Gibbs Racing, having replaced Dale Jarrett, who had left to join Robert Yates's operation. Labonte's victory came in his third full season in NASCAR's Cup series.

The thirty-one-year-old Labonte cruised to a 6.27-second victory over his older brother, Terry, after Ken Schrader's car experienced late race engine problems. He had started the race on the outside of the front row beside Jeff Gordon. During the event, which had seven caution flags for thirty-three laps, Labonte led six times for eighty-five laps, including the final forty-three.

It would be a new millennium before another first-time winner would appear in Charlotte Motor Speedway's Victory Lane. Matt Kenseth, driving a Jack Roush–owned Ford, fought off Bobby Labonte to become the first rookie ever to win the Coca-Cola 600.

With the threat of rain in the air at the race's beginning, Dale Earnhardt Jr. quickly made it clear that he intended to back up his first victory in the All-Star race a week earlier. He would lead 175 of the 400 laps before having to settle for fourth in the race that was stopped for nearly an hour due to rain.

A caution with 40 laps remaining in stock car racing's longest race provided Kenseth with the opportunity he needed to challenge for the victory. Crew chief Robbie Reiser ordered a right-rear tire air pressure adjustment on Kenseth's Ford Taurus when he pitted with the other lead-lap cars. The task was quickly accomplished, and Kenseth returned to the race in third. When the race restarted, Kenseth's Ford responded. He fought past Dale Earnhardt Jr. to claim second on lap 369 and then moved into first by passing Bobby Labonte on lap 375. Labonte never challenged Kenseth again, finishing a half second behind him.

Dale Earnhardt took third, Dale Earnhardt Jr. fourth and Dale Jarrett fifth.

Slightly more than two years later, in the October 2002 race, Jamie McMurray shocked everyone by corralling his first-ever NASCAR Cup victory in only his second start. The twenty-six-year-old McMurray was substituting for Sterling Marlin, who had broken his neck in an accident at Kansas Speedway two weeks earlier while leading the points.

McMurray was ecstatic and didn't even attempt to contain his excitement during his lengthy post-race interview in the Charlotte Motor Speedway press box. He hadn't even visited Victory Lane in two Busch Series (now Nationwide) seasons. Now he possessed a victory at Charlotte, a place he didn't even want to be two weeks earlier because of past performances at the track. In fact, McMurray admitted waking up at 4:00 a.m. drenched in sweat and worrying about causing problems in the event for other drivers. He told reporters he simply wanted to finish the race and avoid making an idiot of himself.

McMurray was consistent throughout the race that was held on a lengthy, rainy day. He led ninety-six of the final one hundred laps to score the victory, which has been considered one of the biggest upsets in NASCAR history. The Missouri driver edged Bobby Labonte by 0.35 of a second for the surprise victory. Rounding out the top five, respectively, were Tony Stewart, Jeff Gordon and Rusty Wallace.

Casey Mears's inaugural NASCAR Sprint Cup victory came in the 2007 Coca-Cola 600, which became a fuel mileage race after two multi-car accidents in the first one hundred miles damaged nearly half the field. In a long night with the race consuming more than four and a half hours, several front-running cars had to pit for fuel in the final ten laps. Actually, the stage was set for a fuel mileage race with fifty-seven laps remaining when some teams said they could make it to the finish and others said they would have to pit.

Tony Stewart had possession of the lead, over Mears and Dale Earnhardt Jr., when Mears began slowing with twenty laps remaining in an effort to save fuel. Jimmie Johnson had to relinquish fourth place with ten laps to go for a splash of fuel. Mark Martin gave up fifth with nine remaining to pit for fuel, and leader Stewart followed on the next lap. Earnhardt Jr. inherited the lead when Stewart pitted but then had to stop as well. Next in line for the lead was Denny Hamlin, but his car needed a drink of fuel with five laps remaining.

Now it was Mears's turn, and he managed to hold on for the victory. His Hendrick Motorsports Chevrolet ran out of fuel during his victory lap. With Mears's victory, all four Hendrick drivers had collected a win in 2007.

Two days of rain played an instrumental role in David Reutimann emerging the victor in the 2009 Coca-Cola 600. Rain on the scheduled race day forced track officials to postpone the event until Monday, the first time in the event's fifty-year history. However, the rain decided to hang around for Memorial Day Monday as well. Intermittent showers that Monday resulted in a race that was constantly being started and stopped. When the sixth caution appeared for rain just 22 laps past the halfway mark in the race, Reutimann and crew chief Rodney Childers decided to remain on the track when leader Kyle Busch led a parade of cars down pit road. Reutimann was fourteenth at the time, but he found himself in the lead with the gamble. He took the lead on lap 222 and led 5 laps under caution—the only time he possessed the number one position the entire day—before NASCAR ordered the field to pit road and issued a red flag due to rain.

Unlike most of the drivers who headed for their motor homes, Reutimann remained with his Michael Waltrip Racing Toyota for two hours and three minutes. Despite the rain, he was joined by his sixty-eight-year-old father, Buzzie, who still competed on dirt at East Bay Raceway near Tampa, Florida. When NASCAR finally declared the rain-shortened race official, Reutimann and his father couldn't believe their dream of a Sprint Cup victory had come true.

During his post-race press conference, an excited Reutimann said,

This is probably one of the greatest days of my life with the exception of the birth of my daughter…when you try so hard and you struggle and things are starting to go your way and then they don't, over a while you maybe come to the point where you're like, "I don't want to get my hopes up and get too pumped up because you don't know what's gonna happen." Now I'm having a hard time relaxing and enjoying the moment.

Buzzie Reutimann noted it had been "a long road."

"It's taken us a long time to get here," the elder Reutimann told the media that rainy day. "I'm afraid I'm going to wake up in the morning and find out I'm dreaming all of this."

It wasn't a dream, however, as all of those who obtained their first Cup victory or pole at Charlotte Motor Speedway discovered when they woke up the morning after their accomplishment. They really had etched their names in the record books as winners.

CHAPTER EIGHT

AHEAD OF ITS TIME

When one hears the name Charlotte Motor Speedway, the word "innovation" usually comes to mind. It was the first track to provide year-round living accommodations with trackside condominiums, the world's largest HD TV screen, VIP suites, a Speedway Club with fine dining and a ballroom, an all-you-can-eat grandstand and a weekly series for youngsters interested in building racing careers.

Bruton Smith has often described himself as a frustrated builder, a person who enjoys creating and watching his visions spring to life.

"That's where Bruton and I, despite the fact things didn't end between us like they should have, where we worked well together," said Wheeler, who retired after the 2008 Coca-Cola 600 following a major rift between him and Smith over the construction of the dragway and Smith's threat to local governments to move Charlotte Motor Speedway out of Cabarrus County. "In those days [when things were going well], he liked to build things. He didn't like to mess with the ordinary, everyday things at the racetrack. He liked building stuff and I did, too. We worked well together doing that."

Of course there were always disagreements. In fact, Wheeler said he and Smith would argue for months over something before reaching a solution. The primary issue would be the amount of money to be spent on a project. Smith was always more grandiose than Wheeler.

"It worked out pretty good the way we would debate what we were going to do," Wheeler continued. "He and I came from the same place. He was brought up on a farm near a small town. I was brought up in a small town.

We knew how working people felt about things. That was and still is who is in the grandstands despite what some press releases say. We knew what these people wanted, what they liked and they didn't like."

A constant argument between Smith and Wheeler was the number of seats to build at the speedway. Smith always wanted to construct more seats than Wheeler.

Watching the metamorphosis of Charlotte Motor Speedway after Smith regained control of the track was intriguing and awesome. When Smith first assumed control, the office hadn't changed since the track opened. It was still a two-story yellow farmhouse, and there was a pecan grove near it where campers would reside on race weekends. By the early 1980s, the speedway's offices had been moved to a structure known as the Goodyear building at the intersection of Highway 29 and Morehead Road. Tickets were sold in a small area at the front entrance, Goodyear stored its racing tires on one side of the building and small race teams were located on the other. The speedway offices were upstairs. Smith always had an office at the track, but he conducted most of his business from his headquarters at his flagship car dealership, Town and Country Ford on Independence Boulevard in east Charlotte. He still maintains an office there today. Ed Griffith, who was a stockholder in the track and a retired corporate executive, always camped in the pecan grove during the May race weeks and was dubbed the "Mayor of Pecan Grove" by his friends.

When Smith regained control of the track, an infield media center didn't exist. Each race weekend, a trailer was pulled into the infield where a reporter could set up a typewriter or the new portable computers that were just starting to be used by daily newspapers. No one ever used it, however, as it made more sense at the beginning of the 1980s to conduct interviews in the garage and then head to the newly constructed press box to write and file stories. When an infield media center finally made it to the drawing board, it included a dark room for each wire service—the Associated Press and United Press International—and the *Charlotte Observer* with each photo department being allowed to design its work area.

The new infield media center, however, was only the tip of the iceberg when it came to the construction plans Bruton Smith had for the track. In 1983, Smith announced a $30 million expansion plan that would take ten years to compete. The plan included condominiums, suites, seats, campgrounds and parking, but it was the condominiums that raised eyebrows and had most people shaking their heads. Who would want a condominium at a racetrack? It didn't make sense. Smith, however, thought it did. Years later, he said

Charlotte Motor Speedway's first condominium complex opened in 1984. *CMS Archives.*

he obtained the idea for the initial condominiums located at the first-turn entrance from tailgaters at college and professional football games. In his mind, he felt the condos were a way to tailgate at a racetrack.

However, the condominiums weren't first on the expansion plan list. That spot belonged to a new tunnel entrance for the original one constructed under the fourth turn, additional spectator parking and a 1.2-mile perimeter beltway around the speedway.

Phase one of the ten-year plan was to be completed prior to the 1984 World 600 at an estimated cost of $10 million. That phase included 12,100 new seats in the Chrysler Grandstand. Other items to be built were thirty new VIP suites, two new elevators to the suite level, a modern catering kitchen and additional parking for five thousand spectator vehicles. The two-bedroom condos fell into this phase and would be constructed above the first-turn Grand National Tower seats. The initial price tag: $120,000. Each condo's living area faced the track. There was a kitchen, dining and living area with a step down to seats located in front of the large window that was on the side of the building facing the track. The bedrooms were on the back side of the condo with windows facing the building's walkway.

Other items in the planning stages were a major campground, modern restroom and shower facilities and extensive landscaping. Speedway officials

The view from the first condominium building constructed outside the speedway's first turn was quite spectacular. *CMS Archives.*

also planned to implement a tram system for the fans, pave more parking areas, add seats, repave the track and construct a new office complex.

The motorsports community had barely recovered from its surprise at the condos' popularity when Smith announced the new seven-story office tower would include a membership club where people could dine, dance and watch races. It would have a beautiful oak bar area, marble accents, a boutique and a ballroom. Darrell Waltrip's membership shows his as the first one, but since the Speedway Club's creation in the 1980s, it has grown to a facility boasting five thousand members. Lunch and dinner are served year round, and the club also plans special events. It has been the site of many wedding receptions, including Ryan and Krissie Newman's, and local high school proms. Three different levels of membership are offered by the Speedway Club: personal, small business and corporate. Race winners are usually taken to the club for a toast after Victory Lane ceremonies and post-race interviews.

Another condominium complex was added between the track's first and second turns in the early 1990s. Identified as the First Turn Condominiums, their initial price ranged from $375,000 to $500,000, and they were larger and more luxurious than those found in the initial forty-unit complex built

The second at-track living quarters constructed by the speedway in the early 1990s were larger and more luxurious than the first complex. They are known as the First Turn Condominiums. *CMS Archives.*

in 1984. Designed by Dennis Yates & Associates and ranging from 1,300 to 1,500 square feet, each condominium featured two bedrooms, two baths, a living area and a kitchen with a seating area for eighteen people.

After winning the 1989 Coca-Cola 600, Darrell Waltrip was transported to the Speedway Club for his victory toast. While there, Waltrip was offered an opportunity to purchase one of the new condos for $75,000.

"I think it was three or four years later they were going for $350,000 to $500,000. I guess I missed it on that one," Waltrip commented.

Bruton Smith never stops designing or thinking about items to build, and that characteristic of his resulted in an architectural rendition of a football stadium on the speedway's frontstretch grassy apron. Smith's idea surfaced in the mid-1980s when Charlotte businessman George Shinn was attempting to bring a World Football League team to the Queen City. Bank of America Stadium didn't exist, and Smith felt the speedway's facilities could fill the void. The seats would be stored in the ground when the field wasn't in use. (When Smith had announced initial plans to build a superspeedway in south Charlotte in 1959, a football stadium was included.)

Bruton Smith envisioned a football field on the speedway's grassy apron that separates the frontstretch from pit road. The grandstands would be stored underground. *CMS Archives*.

By the time Smith headed into the second decade of the twenty-first century, he had decided it was time for Charlotte Motor Speedway to have a $200 million renovation. The first phase was launched with the installation of 22,850 new seats along the frontstretch. The original concrete bleachers became the foundation for the new grandstands constructed directly over them. Where fans once sat on concrete, stadium-style seats now exist. The new structure includes more than one million pounds of steel and aluminum. It features twenty-inch-wide seats, and the width of each row has been increased to give fans additional leg room. Handrails were added down the center of each aisle. While the grandstand structure and seats were new, the green metal uprights supporting nearly 20,000 of the seat backs and bottoms were recycled from the Charlotte Coliseum, which was open from 1988 to 2005.

While Charlotte Motor Speedway has set the industry standard in construction, that isn't the only area where it has been a leader. Its elaborate pre-race shows and promotional techniques have been a mainstay since the 1980s. In fact, they are the reason Humpy Wheeler still carries the nickname the "P.T. Barnum of Racing." Before Jay Howard worked at the speedway with Wheeler and later formed JHE Productions in order to produce the shows, Wheeler would meet with the speedway's communications department to discuss ideas. However, he knew an idea could spring from anywhere. Such was the case with the Great American Taxi Cab Race, an event that Wheeler maintains would exist today if it weren't for an article in *Sports Illustrated*.

During the last three decades, Charlotte Motor Speedway has become famous for its extravagant pre-race shows. They have ranged from a circus to the reenactment of the invasion of Grenada. *CMS Archives*.

Wheeler conceived the idea in 1979 while meeting with CBS Sports executives in New York about televising the World 600. Network executives told Wheeler they would consider covering the race live if the track could come up with some other type of programming they could broadcast. Wheeler's first suggestion was Saturday's three-hundred-mile race. They declined. Then he suggested a motorcycle jump due to Evel Knievel's popularity. They didn't bite on that one either.

"I thought of about five other things, and I couldn't get them to blink," Wheeler recalled. "I thought, okay, I'm in New York; they've got to like something to do in New York City."

That's when it hit Wheeler—taxicabs. They love to hate taxicabs. He then looked at the executives and proposed the Great American Taxi Cab Race.

"You don't want to give anything away when you're negotiating, but I could see that I hit a cord," Wheeler said.

Wheeler developed the event's concept during the meeting. They would take the best cab drivers from major cities, such as New York, Chicago and Los Angeles, put them in taxicabs and have them race down pit road and around the frontstretch. A hotel would be erected so that they'd have to stop and pick up a suitcase, and there would be a tollbooth installed on pit road. To determine the participants, a slalom course would be set up in a Sears store parking lot in each city on a designated day. Cab drivers would then execute the course, with the winner receiving a trip to Charlotte Motor Speedway and a chance to participate in the event.

"They bit, hook, line and sinker," Wheeler said. "They thought it was the best idea they'd ever heard. I was feeling pretty good until I got to the elevator and then I thought, 'How am I going to put this damn thing together?'"

Wheeler immediately contacted the American Taxi Cab Association in Washington, D.C., and the organization liked the idea. It wouldn't provide any financial backing, but it pledged the speedway its support and cooperation. It would assist speedway officials with contacting the various cab companies. Sears agreed to the program in every city except for New York. Those cab drivers had to go to Islip (New York) Speedway to run its slalom course. Wheeler hired Bob Latford, a former public relations director for the speedway, to oversee the project. Now they needed cars for the cabbies to drive in the Charlotte competition.

"People were getting rid of their big cars, so I got my brother, David, and gave him $10,000 to $12,000. We put an ad in the paper for them to bring their big car to the speedway and get cash for it," Wheeler explained. He continued to tell how the car-buying procedure worked:

> We were in the Goodyear building then, and I could look on the parking area from my office window. They would drive under my window, and I would look at the car from there. David would check out the car. If it was top notch, he would hold up three fingers, two if it was good and one if we didn't want it. I would then give him a prearranged signal if I wanted him to buy the car. People kept bringing these really nice cars. In one afternoon we bought twenty-four cars.

Wheeler then sent the cars across the street to former NASCAR driver D.K. Ulrich's race shop, where they were prepared for the event. He put one roll bar in them; painted them yellow, checker or some other color; and put a yellow cab light on top and the name of the cab company the driver was representing on the side. The participants arrived on Friday so they could practice for Saturday's event. Wheeler also enlisted former NASCAR driver Roy Tyner to be the event's "police officer."

"We bought an old highway patrol car that was still black and silver and put a siren on top of it," Wheeler recalled. "We got a motor that really would honk and we put soft tires on it. He could go anywhere on the track he wanted to go. He would run down the cab drivers, pull them over and make them sit there for ten seconds. That proved to be a real hoot because it made him the bad guy."

Wheeler said they knew everyone would hate Tyner by the end of the event, so they wanted to do something no one expected. They put a jump stop (a device used to flip cars in the movies) in the grassy apron and painted it green so no one could see it. The event would end with Tyner charging off the fourth turn through the grass, hitting the stop and flipping. It worked perfectly.

"It was total mayhem and funny as the devil, which was what we wanted," Wheeler said with a chuckle. "On the first lap they tore down the toll booth. People were trying to make stops and slamming into the back of each other. Then they tore down the hotel and there was debris everywhere."

Bill Connell, the track's public address announcer for about two decades, provided constant commentary for the event that often resembled a Keystone Kop act. Wheeler had always told Connell there should never be any dead air time on the PA, and this time, Connell's talents, along with the cabbies' antics, kept the crowd laughing.

"Unfortunately for us, one of the networks did the world belly flop championships that same day," Wheeler said. He continued:

> *They were all on one-week delays. Well,* Sports Illustrated, *in all of its great, pontifical bearing, did an editorial the next week on trash sports. It ripped this network for the world belly flop championships and said it had no place on TV. Then, in the last paragraph, they said, "Oh, yes, another one almost as bad at Charlotte, the Great American Taxi Cab race." The networks put their starched shirts on the next week and declared they weren't going to televise trash sports anymore. Now, it's been relegated to great popularity on the cable systems.*

During Wheeler's tenure at the track, he learned no idea was stupid because while someone might not be creative, it didn't mean he couldn't recognize creativity. Such was the case when the speedway settled on Robosaurus for pre-race entertainment. A secretary at the speedway had seen the thirty-ton, fire-breathing, transforming T-Rex that eats cars in the *National Enquirer.* While others at the track had brushed her off, Wheeler listened, looked at the photos and decided children attending the race on Saturday would enjoy it.

"Other than the school bus jump, that was probably the funniest thing that worked the best of anything we did," Wheeler said. "Kids, especially

Fireball Roberts signs autographs for Boy Scouts attending a race at Charlotte Motor Speedway in the early 1960s. *CMS Archives.*

kids in the first and second grade, loved the school bus jump, and I finally figured out why. They think if you tear up enough school buses, there won't be any left and they won't have to go to school."

From the beginning, speedway management realized the value of getting children interested in the sport. Drivers would go into the grandstands in the early 1960s and sign autographs for Boy Scouts, some pre-race shows were designed with children in mind and a Kids Zone was recently created near the speedway's entrance. Charlotte Motor Speedway also was the first track to create a mascot—Lug Nut—and a racing series for aspiring drivers. Known as the Summer Shootout, children can get a taste for racing in Bandoleros and Legends cars. Wheeler created 600 Racing that manufactures Bandoleros, Legends and Thunder Roadsters while serving as the speedway's president and general manager.

"That's probably the thing I miss the most right now," Wheeler reflects about the cars that are now marketed internationally. "It was the only successful effort to mass produce race cars that's ever been made."

Even though the speedway wasn't well received in the community in the mid-1970s, when Smith and Wheeler took over the track, its attitude changed over the years as the speedway worked to provide events and activities for the local area. Speedway employees traveled to Indianapolis in the early 1980s to study the events that existed in that city during its month of speed. The result was the 600 Festival. Each year, the previous winner of the 600 was honored at a nice dinner funded by Unocal; the Festival of Lights parade was implemented; and the 600 Children's Charities Ball, a black tie affair, was created. The dinner ended when Unocal left the sport at the end of the 2003 season. The Festival of Lights parade was discontinued after about a decade, but Food Lion Speed Street, which had been created, remained.

Even though there is no longer a black tie affair during Coca-Cola 600 week, the Speedway Children's Charities remain with a chapter at each Speedway Motorsports Incorporated track. Speedway Children's Charities was founded by Bruton Smith and his former wife, Bonnie, as a memoriam and legacy to their son, Bruton Cameron Smith, who was only a few months old when he died of crib death. The charity became a national organization in 1982, but each chapter determines the needs of children in its community. The children are helped directly with everything from educational support to something as simple as a coat or a meal.

In the late 1980s and early 1990s, the speedway also worked diligently with the schools, organizing and hosting motorsports career days at middle and high schools. The effort was the result of a program developed by then special events supervisor Susan Russo. Known as "Racing in the Classroom," the program was designed to motivate students by taking an inside look at NASCAR racing. By using NASCAR racing as a base, the program was designed to show the students how the sport could be applied to math, English, art, geography and science.

Another speedway creation that exists today is the annual media tour, which hosts motorsports writers and broadcasters for a week each January, when they visit race shops and talk with competitors. Conceived by Ed Clark and Bob Kelly, the tour originally was based on the former Atlantic Coast Conference football writers' tour. That event no longer exists, but the

Dale Earnhardt talks to reporters attending the Charlotte Motor Speedway Media Tour in the mid-1980s. Team owner Richard Childress leans against the race car. *CMS Archives.*

Charlotte Motor Speedway Media Tour is still quite popular and now hosts international media.

The inaugural tour in 1983 lasted three days, and in that time, the media visited fifteen different race shops. Each day began at sunrise and didn't wind down until midnight. This outstanding contribution to the sport of stock car racing netted Charlotte Motor Speedway the prestigious Myers Brothers Award in 1984. The award is given annually by the National Motorsports Press Association to the individual or organization that has provided outstanding contributions to stock car racing.

No writing time was allotted on the inaugural tour. However, it does exist now and is built into each afternoon so stories can be filed before the evening media event begins. Today's electronic devices allow for writing and filing on buses as the media travels from one event to another. Also, thanks to social media, there's a constant flow of information to fans from the four-day tour.

Charlotte Motor Speedway officials have also occasionally provided non-business services for the racing community. When NASCAR drivers Tim Richmond and Rob Moroso died, the speedway hosted memorial services for the motorsports community in the Smith Tower ballroom. It provided the same type of service one May during the week leading into the Coca-Cola 600 so people could pay their condolences to Leonard Wood, who

When Charlotte Motor Speedway was given the Myers Brothers Award in 1984, members of the track's staff went to New York City to accept the honor at the Waldorf-Astoria Hotel. They were, from the left, Ron Swaim, Ed Clark, Carolyn Rudd, Bruton Smith, Humpy Wheeler, Carolyn Carrier, Darlene Dixon and Jim Duncan. *CMS Archives.*

lost his wife in a car wreck. The accident occurred when the family was returning home to Stuart, Virginia, after Michael Waltrip drove the Wood Brothers Ford to victory in the 1996 All-Star race.

When North Carolina farmers were on the verge of losing their herds due to a severe drought in 1986, Charlotte Motor Speedway served as a staging area for what became known as the "Hayride 500." It was an off-weekend for the race teams, so the team hauler drivers obtained numerous tractor-trailers, formed a convoy and headed to Ohio to bring hundreds of bales of hay back to the state's starving livestock. Then North Carolina governor James G. Martin started the convoy by waving the green flag. Richard Petty appeared for the event, as did then North Carolina agriculture commissioner Jim Graham. The only NASCAR driver who took time off to travel with the convoy was Tim Richmond, an Ohio native. At the end of the year, the National Motorsports Press Association presented its prestigious Myers Brothers Award to the Hayride 500.

Ever since Charlotte Motor Speedway was created, it has been the cornerstone of Bruton Smith's motorsports empire, his flagship track.

Tim Richmond was the only NASCAR driver to make the round trip with the "Hayride 500." Attending the start of the event, from the left, were North Carolina agriculture commissioner Jim Graham, Bruton Smith, North Carolina governor James G. Martin and RJR employee Steve Tucker. *CMS Archives.*

However, when Speedway Motorsports Incorporated became the first motorsports company offered on the New York Stock Exchange, things began changing for the historic facility. Not only did Wheeler have to focus on the day-to-day activities at Charlotte, but he was also now SMI's president, and he was constantly traveling to Europe on business trips.

"We only had Atlanta at the time we went public," Wheeler said about the initial offering on February 24, 1995. "We knew to expand it would necessitate going public, but up until that time, the emphasis had always been on the Cup series and making Charlotte a showplace. We had our eye on Bristol, and Bruton really had his eye on Texas. He loved Texas. The only place he liked more than Texas was Las Vegas."

He continued to explain SMI's method of expansion:

> *After we went public and we got the initial funds, the emphasis shifted away from Charlotte. Not much money was spent at Charlotte after that. Most of the money went into buying Bristol, redoing it and building Texas. Huge, huge amounts of money went into Texas. We ended up with $350*

million in Texas. At that time, it was the most money ever spent on any
speedway in the world. Then we spent $48 million on revamping Sears
Point. We got into a debate a lot about that track.

Smith's Speedway Motorsports Incorporated, now headed by himself
and his son Marcus, owns eight tracks, but Charlotte Motor Speedway is
still the foundation for the family empire. At age thirty-four, Marcus Smith
replaced Humpy Wheeler as the track's president and general manager
when Wheeler retired.

The younger Smith began preparing for his current position while
in junior high, working at the track during the summer picking up trash,
trimming weeds, painting walls and performing other outside maintenance
duties. He also spent his summers working as an intern in several Charlotte
Motor Speedway departments, including tickets, events, public relations,
administration and corporate sales.

In 1996, Marcus Smith joined the speedway's corporate sales department
as a marketing assistant and was eventually promoted to account executive.
He spearheaded the effort to form SMI's national sales and marketing
department and later was named to head the new effort, becoming
the manager of new business development for Speedway Motorsports
Incorporated in 1999.

In 2001, Smith was promoted to SMI vice-president of business
development. Three years later, he became a SMI director and was promoted
to executive vice-president of national sales and marketing, working on
behalf of the company's eleven motorsports-related operating units: eight
speedways, Performance Racing Network, SMI Properties and U.S. Legend
Cars International.

In addition to overseeing Charlotte Motor Speedway, the young Smith is
also president and chief operating officer of SMI, president of Speedway
Children's Charities Charlotte chapter and a board member of Motor
Racing Outreach and Youth Commission International.

Since Marcus Smith assumed his current position, the world's largest
HD TV has been installed on the backstretch between turns two and three.
The screen measures two hundred feet wide, stands eighty feet tall, weighs
165,000 pounds and covers sixteen thousand square feet. The auto fair that
was begun in the 1980s continues to operate on two three-day weekends—
one in the spring, the other in the fall—and a Christmas light show has been
added during the holiday season. From Thanksgiving until New Year's, the
speedway's garage area becomes a Christmas village.

In the nearly forty years since Bruton Smith returned to North Carolina to reclaim his beloved Charlotte Motor Speedway, his life has undergone some drastic changes. He was broke when he left the Tar Heel State in the early 1960s but returned with a plan that allowed him to regain ownership of Charlotte Motor Speedway and turn the farm boy from Stanly County, North Carolina, into a millionaire.

"It has been wonderful," Bruton Smith told the media during a press conference the weekend of the Coca-Cola 600's fiftieth anniversary. "I think [Charlotte] Motor Speedway is the crown jewel. I'm just pleased to have a part here. Was it easy? No it wasn't, and I would not go back through it for anything."

RACE RESULTS

NASCAR Sprint Cup Series

1960

June 19 World 600
Winner, Joe Lee Johnson, Chevrolet
Time of Race: 5:34:06
Average Speed: 107.735 mph
Pole Speed: 133.904 mph (Fireball
    Roberts, Pontiac)

Cautions: 8 for 45 laps
Margin of Victory: 4 laps
Lead Changes: 11

October 16 National 400
Winner, Speedy Thompson, Ford
Time of Race: 3:32:50
Average Speed: 112.905 mph
Pole Speed: 133.465 mph (Fireball
    Roberts, Pontiac)

Cautions: 7 for 34 laps
Margin of Victory: 1 lap
Lead Changes: 8

1961

May 28 World 600
Winner, David Pearson, Pontiac

Time of Race: 5:22:29
Average Speed: 111.633 mph
Pole Speed: 131.611 mph (Richard
   Petty, Plymouth)

Cautions: 7 for 57 laps
Margin of Victory: 2 laps
Lead Changes: 17

October 15 National 400
Winner, Joe Weatherly, Pontiac
Time of Race: 3:20:20
Average Speed: 119.95 mph

Cautions: 3 for 18 laps
Margin of Victory: 1.5 car
   lengths

Pole Speed: 138.577 mph (David
   Pearson, Pontiac)

Lead Changes: 13

1962

May 27 World 600
Winner, Nelson Stacy, Ford
Time of Race: 4:46:44
Average Speed: 125.552 mph

Cautions: 2 for 14 laps
Margin of Victory: 32.35
   seconds

Pole Speed: 140.15 mph (Fireball
   Roberts, Pontiac)

Lead Changes: 18

October 14 National 400
Winner, Junior Johnson, Pontiac
Time of Race: 3:01:42
Average Speed: 132.085 mph
Pole Speed: 140.287 mph (Fireball
   Roberts, Pontiac)

Cautions: 1 for 6 laps
Margin of Victory: 2 laps
Lead Changes: 10

1963

June 2 World 600
Winner, Fred Lorenzen, Ford
Time of Race: 4:31:52
Average Speed: 132.417 mph

Cautions: 2 for 14 laps
Margin of Victory: 35
   seconds

Pole Speed: 141.148 mph (Junior
   Johnson, Chevrolet)

Lead Changes: 15

October 13 National 400
Winner, Junior Johnson, Chevrolet
Time of Race: 3:01:54
Average Speed: 132.105 mph

Pole Speed: 143.017 mph (Fred
  Lorenzen, Ford)

Cautions: 3 for 17 laps
Margin of Victory: 12
  seconds
Lead Changes: 14

1964

May 24 World 600
Winner, Jim Paschal, Plymouth
Time of Race: 4:46:14
Average Speed: 125.772 mph
Pole Speed: 144.346 mph (Jimmy
  Pardue, Plymouth)

Cautions: 7 for 48 laps
Margin of Victory: 4 laps
Lead Changes: 14

October 18 National 400
Winner, Fred Lorenzen, Ford
Time of Race: 2:58:35
Average Speed: 134.475 mph
Pole Speed: 150.711 mph (Richard
  Petty, Plymouth)

Cautions: 4 for 21 laps
Margin of Victory: 1 lap
Lead Changes: 10

1965

May 23 World 600
Winner, Fred Lorenzen, Ford
Time of Race: 4:55:38
Average Speed: 121.722 mph
Pole Speed: 145.268 mph (Fred Lorenzen, Ford)

Cautions: 11 for 80 laps
Margin of Victory: 6.4 laps
Lead Changes: 22

October 17 National 400
Winner, Fred Lorenzen, Ford
Time of Race: 3:21:44
Average Speed: 119.117 mph

Pole Speed: 147.773 mph (Fred
  Lorenzen, Ford)

Cautions: 6 for 47 laps
Margin of Victory: 3 car
  lengths
Lead Changes: 28

1966

May 22 World 600
Winner, Marvin Panch, Plymouth
Time of Race: 4:26:35
Average Speed: 135.042 mph
Pole Speed: 148.637 mph (Richard
  Petty, Plymouth)

Cautions: 5 for 18 laps
Margin of Victory: 2 laps
Lead Changes: 14

October 16 National 500
Winner, LeeRoy Yarbrough
Time of Race: 3:49:55
Average Speed: 130.576 mph

Pole Speed: 150.533 mph (Fred
  Lorenzen, Ford)

Cautions: 6 for 46 laps
Margin of Victory: 18
  seconds
Lead Changes: 14

1967

May 28 World 600
Winner, Jim Paschal, Plymouth
Time of Race: 4:25:02
Average Speed: 135.832 mph
Pole Speed: 154.385 mph (Cale
  Yarborough, Ford)

Cautions: 8 for 32 laps
Margin of Victory: 5 seconds
Lead Changes: 11

October 15 National 500
Winner, Buddy Baker, Dodge
Time of Race: 3:50:04
Average Speed: 130.317 mph
Pole Speed: 154.872 mph (Cale
  Yarborough, Ford)

Cautions: 9 for 64 laps
Margin of Victory: 1 lap
Lead Changes: 22

1968

May 26 World 600
Winner, Buddy Baker, Dodge
Time of Race: 3:04:14
Average Speed: 104.207 mph

Cautions: 6 for 110 laps
Margin of Victory: Under
  caution

Pole Speed: 159.223 mph (Donnie Allison, Ford)

Lead Changes: 16

October 20 National 500
Winner, Charlie Glotzbach, Dodge
Time of Race: 3:42:08
Average Speed: 135.234 mph

Cautions: 6 for 49 laps
Margin of Victory: 7 seconds

Pole Speed: 156.06 mph (Charlie Glotzbach, Dodge)

Lead Changes: 26

1969

May 25 World 600
Winner, LeeRoy Yarbrough, Mercury
Time of Race: 4:27:56
Average Speed: 134.361 mph
Pole Speed: 159.296 mph (Donnie Allison, Ford)

Cautions: 5 for 45 laps
Margin of Victory: 2 laps
Lead Changes: 13

October 12 National 500
Winner, Donnie Allison, Ford
Time of Race: 3:48:32
Average Speed: 131.271 mph

Cautions: 9 for 50 laps
Margin of Victory: 16 seconds

Pole Speed: 162.162 mph (Cale Yarborough, Mercury)

Lead Changes: 28

1970

May 24 World 600
Winner, Donnie Allison, Ford
Time of Race: 4:37:36
Average Speed: 129.68 mph
Pole Speed: 159.277 mph (Bobby Isaac, Dodge)

Cautions: 10 for 66 laps
Margin of Victory: 2 laps
Lead Changes: 28

October 11 National 500
Winner, LeeRoy Yarbrough, Mercury
Time of Race: 4:03:28

Cautions: 8 for 63 laps

Average Speed: 123.246 mph

Margin of Victory: Under caution

Pole Speed: 157.273 mph (Charlie Glotzbach, Dodge)

Lead Changes: 23

1971

May 30 World 600
Winner, Bobby Allison, Mercury
Time of Race: 4:16:20
Average Speed: 140.422 mph

Cautions: 3 for 24 laps
Margin of Victory: 33.9 seconds

Pole Speed: 157.788 mph (Charlie Glotzbach, Chevrolet)

Lead Changes: 13

October 10 National 500
Winner, Bobby Allison, Mercury
Time of Race: 2:49:38
Average Speed: 126.14 mph
Pole Speed: 157.085 mph (Charlie Glotzbach, Chevrolet)

Cautions: 6 for 37 laps
Margin of Victory: 5 seconds
Lead Changes: 10

1972

May 28 World 600
Winner, Buddy Baker, Dodge
Time of Race: 4:13:04
Average Speed: 142.255 mph

Cautions: 3 for 24 laps
Margin of Victory: 23.7 seconds

Pole Speed: 158.162 mph (Bobby Allison, Chevrolet)

Lead Changes: 22

October 8 National 500
Winner, Bobby Allison, Chevrolet
Time of Race: 3:45:37
Average Speed: 133.234 mph

Cautions: 6 for 40 laps
Margin of Victory: 2 car lengths

Pole Speed: 158.539 mph (David Pearson, Mercury)

Lead Changes: 21

1973

May 27 World 600
Winner, Buddy Baker, Dodge
Time of Race: 4:26:53
Average Speed: 134.89 mph

Pole Speed: 158.051 mph (Buddy
Baker, Dodge)

Cautions: 6 for 48 laps
Margin of Victory: 1.8
seconds
Lead Changes: 23

October 7 National 500
Winner, Cale Yarborough, Chevrolet
Time of Race: 3:26:58
Average Speed: 145.24 mph

Pole Speed: 158.315 mph (David
Pearson, Mercury)

Cautions: 2 for 16 laps
Margin of Victory: 1.4
seconds
Lead Changes: 12

1974

May 26 World 600
Winner, David Pearson, Mercury
Time of Race: 3:58:21
Average Speed: 135.72 mph

Pole Speed: 157.498 mph (David
Pearson, Mercury)

Cautions: 8 for 48 laps
Margin of Victory: 0.6
second
Lead Changes: 37

October 6 National 500
Winner, David Pearson, Mercury
Time of Race: 4:10:41
Average Speed: 119.912 mph

Pole Speed: 158.749 mph (David
Pearson, Mercury)

Cautions: 9 for 79 laps
Margin of Victory: 1.4
seconds
Lead Changes: 47

1975

May 25 World 600
Winner, Richard Petty, Dodge
Time of Race: 4:07:42
Average Speed: 145.327 mph
Pole Speed: 159.353 mph (David
  Pearson, Mercury)

Cautions: 3 for 12 laps
Margin of Victory: 1 lap
Lead Changes: 17

October 5 National 500
Winner, Richard Petty, Dodge
Time of Race: 3:47:22
Average Speed: 132.209 mph

Pole Speed: 161.701 mph (David
  Pearson, Mercury)

Cautions: 7 for 53 laps
Margin of Victory: 0.26
  second
Lead Changes: 29

1976

May 30 World 600
Winner, David Pearson, Mercury
Time of Race: 4:22:06
Average Speed: 137.352 mph

Pole Speed: 159.132 mph (David
  Pearson, Mercury)

Cautions: 7 for 38 laps
Margin of Victory: Under
  caution
Lead Changes: 37

October 10 National 500
Winner, Donnie Allison, Chevrolet
Time of Race: 3:32:51
Average Speed: 141.226 mph

Pole Speed: 161.223 mph (David
  Pearson, Mercury)

Cautions: 3 for 18 laps
Margin of Victory: 12.2
  seconds
Lead Changes: 26

1977

May 29 World 600
Winner, Richard Petty, Dodge

Time of Race: 4:21:29

Average Speed: 137.676 mph

Pole Speed: 161.435 mph (David
Pearson, Mercury)

Cautions: 6 for 31 laps

Margin of Victory: 30.8
seconds

Lead Changes: 25

October 9 National 500
Winner, Benny Parsons, Chevrolet
Time of Race: 3:30:32

Average Speed: 142.78 mph

Pole Speed: 160.892 mph (David
Pearson, Mercury)

Cautions: 4 for 18 laps

Margin of Victory: 19.2
seconds

Lead Changes: 18

1978

May 28 World 600
Winner, Darrell Waltrip, Chevrolet
Time of Race: 4:20:12

Average Speed: 138.355 mph

Pole Speed: 160.551 mph (David
Pearson, Mercury)

Cautions: 6 for 32 laps

Margin of Victory: 2 seconds

Lead Changes: 43

October 8 NAPA National 500
Winner, Bobby Allison, Ford
Time of Race: 3:31:57

Average Speed: 141.826 mph

Pole Speed: 161.355 mph (David
Pearson, Mercury)

Cautions: 4 for 21 laps

Margin of Victory: 30.2
seconds

Lead Changes: 40

1979

May 27 World 600
Winner, Darrell Waltrip, Chevrolet
Time of Race: 4:23:24

Average Speed: 136.674 mph

Pole Speed: 160.125 mph (Neil
Bonnett, Mercury)

Cautions: 9 for 48 laps

Margin of Victory: 5.6
seconds

Lead Changes: 54

October 7 NAPA National 500
Winner, Cale Yarborough, Chevrolet
Time of Race: 3:43:53
Average Speed: 134.266 mph
Pole Speed: 164.304 mph (Neil
  Bonnett, Mercury)

Cautions: 8 for 40 laps
Margin of Victory: 1 lap
Lead Changes: 28

1980

May 25 World 600
Winner, Benny Parsons, Chevrolet
Time of Race: 5:01:51
Average Speed: 119.265 mph

Cautions: 14 for 113 laps
Margin of Victory: 0.5
  second

Pole Speed: 165.194 mph (Cale
  Yarborough, Chevrolet)

Lead Changes: 47

October 5 National 500
Winner, Dale Earnhardt, Chevrolet
Time of Race: 3:42:18
Average Speed: 135.243 mph

Cautions: 8 for 44 laps
Margin of Victory: 1.83
  seconds

Pole Speed: 165.634 mph (Buddy Baker, Buick)

Lead Changes: 43

1981

May 24 World 600
Winner, Bobby Allison, Buick
Time of Race: 4:38:22
Average Speed: 129.326 mph

Cautions: 7 for 50 laps
Margin of Victory: 8.2
  seconds

Pole Speed: 158.115 mph (Neil Bonnett, Ford)

Lead Changes: 32

October 11 National 500
Winner, Darrell Waltrip, Buick
Time of Race: 4:15:52
Average Speed: 117.483 mph

Cautions: 12 for 78 laps
Margin of Victory: 31.8
  seconds

Pole Speed: 162.744 mph (Darrell Waltrip, Buick)

Lead Changes: 27

1982

May 30 World 600
Winner, Neil Bonnett, Ford
Time of Race: 4:36:48
Average Speed: 130.058 mph

Cautions: 10 for 62 laps
Margin of Victory: 2 car lengths

Pole Speed: 162.511 mph (David Pearson, Buick)

Lead Changes: 47

October 10 National 500
Winner, Harry Gant, Buick
Time of Race: 3:39:05
Average Speed: 137.208 mph

Cautions: 6 for 34 laps
Margin of Victory: 2.93 seconds

Pole Speed: 164.694 mph (Fireball Roberts, Pontiac)

Lead Changes: 12

1983

May 29 World 600
Winner, Neil Bonnett, Chevrolet
Time of Race: 4:15:51
Average Speed: 140.707 mph

Cautions: 5 for 28 laps
Margin of Victory: 0.8 second

Pole Speed: 162.841 mph (Buddy Baker, Ford)

Lead Changes: 23

October 9 Miller High Life 500
Winner, Richard Petty, Pontiac
Time of Race: 3:34:43
Average Speed: 139.998 mph

Cautions: 8 for 35 laps
Margin of Victory: 3.1 seconds

Pole Speed: 163.073 mph (Tim Richmond, Pontiac)

Lead Changes: 30

1984

May 27 World 600
Winner, Bobby Allison, Buick
Time of Race: 4:38:34
Average Speed: 129.233 mph

Pole Speed: 162.496 mph (Harry
 Gant, Chevrolet)

Cautions: 5 for 48 laps
Margin of Victory: 17
 seconds
Lead Changes: 22

October 7 Miller High Life
Winner, Bill Elliott, Ford
Time of Race: 3:24:41
Average Speed: 148.861 mph

Pole Speed: 165.579 mph (Benny
 Parsons, Chevrolet)

Cautions: 3 for 15 laps
Margin of Victory: 14.5
 seconds
Lead Changes: 22

1985

May 26 Coca-Cola World 600
Winner, Darrell Waltrip, Chevrolet
Time of Race: 4:13:52
Average Speed: 141.807 mph

Pole Speed: 164.703 mph (Bill Elliott, Ford)

Cautions: 7 for 34 laps
Margin of Victory: 14.64
 seconds
Lead Changes: 29

October 6 Miller High Life 500
Winner, Cale Yarborough, Ford
Time of Race: 3:39:48
Average Speed: 136.761 mph

Pole Speed: 166.139 mph (Harry
 Gant, Chevrolet)

Cautions: 6 for 41 laps
Margin of Victory: 1
 second
Lead Changes: 15

1986

May 25 Coca-Cola 600
Winner, Dale Earnhardt, Chevrolet

Time of Race: 4:16:24

Average Speed: 140.406 mph

Pole Speed: 164.511 mph (Geoffrey
 Bodine, Chevrolet)

Cautions: 6 for 32 laps

Margin of Victory: 1.59
 seconds

Lead Changes: 38

October 5 Oakwood Homes 500
Winner, Dale Earnhardt, Chevrolet
Time of Race: 3:47:02

Average Speed: 132.403 mph

Pole Speed: 167.078 mph (Tim
 Richmond, Chevrolet)

Cautions: 6 for 44 laps

Margin of Victory: 1.9
 seconds

Lead Changes: 26

1987

May 24 Coca-Cola 600
Winner, Kyle Petty, Ford
Time of Race: 4:33:48
Average Speed: 131.483 mph
Pole Speed: 170.901 mph (Bill Elliott, Ford)

Cautions: 12 for 68 laps
Margin of Victory: 1 lap
Lead Changes: 23

October 11 Oakwood Homes 500
Winner, Bill Elliott, Ford
Time of Race: 3:54:02

Average Speed: 128.443 mph

Pole Speed: 171.636 mph (Bobby
 Allison, Buick)

Cautions: 7 for 59 laps

Margin of Victory: 2.22
 seconds

Lead Changes: 29

1988

May 29 Coca-Cola 600
Winner, Darrell Waltrip, Chevrolet
Time of Race: 4:49:15

Average Speed: 124.46 mph

Pole Speed: 173.594 mph (Davey Allison, Ford)

Cautions: 13 for 89 laps

Margin of Victory: 0.24
 second

Lead Changes: 43

October 9 Oakwood Homes 500
Winner, Rusty Wallace, Pontiac
Time of Race: 3:50:02
Average Speed: 130.677 mph

Cautions: 10 for 63 laps
Margin of Victory: 1 car
 length

Pole Speed: 175.896 mph (Alan Kulwicki, Ford)

Lead Changes: 36

1989

May 28 Coca-Cola 600
Winner, Darrell Waltrip, Chevrolet
Time of Race: 4:09:52
Average Speed: 144.077 mph

Cautions: 7 for 36 laps
Margin of Victory: 0.99
 second

Pole Speed: 173.021 mph (Alan Kulwicki, Ford)

Lead Changes: 22

October 8 All Pro Auto Parts 500
Winner, Ken Schrader, Chevrolet
Time of Race: 3:20:35
Average Speed: 149.863 mph

Cautions: 4 for 21 laps
Margin of Victory: 3.75
 seconds

Pole Speed: 174.081 mph (Bill Elliott, Ford)

Lead Changes: 19

1990

May 27 World 600
Winner, Rusty Wallace, Pontiac
Time of Race: 4:21:32
Average Speed: 137.65 mph

Cautions: 11 for 48 laps
Margin of Victory: 0.17
 second

Pole Speed: 173.963 mph (Ken
 Schrader, Chevrolet)

Lead Changes: 15

October 7 Mello Yello 500
Winner, Davey Allison, Ford
Time of Race: 3:38:44
Average Speed: 137.428 mph

Cautions: 6 for 37 laps
Margin of Victory: 2.59
 seconds

Pole Speed: 174.385 mph (Brett Bodine, Buick)

Lead Changes: 14

1991

May 26 Coca-Cola 600
Winner, Davey Allison, Ford
Time of Race: 4:19:05

Cautions: 9 for 54 laps

Average Speed: 138.951 mph

Margin of Victory: 1.28 seconds

Pole Speed: 174.82 mph (Mark Martin, Ford)

Lead Changes: 22

October 6 Mello Yello 500
Winner, Geoffrey Bodine, Ford
Time of Race: 3:36:17

Cautions: 6 for 38 laps

Average Speed: 138.984 mph

Margin of Victory: 11.28 seconds

Pole Speed: 176.499 mph (Mark Martin, Ford)

Lead Changes: 10

1992

May 24 Coca-Cola 600
Winner, Dale Earnhardt, Chevrolet
Time of Race: 4:30:43

Cautions: 12 for 62 laps

Average Speed: 132.98 mph

Margin of Victory: 0.41 second

Pole Speed: 175.479 mph (Bill Elliott, Ford)

Lead Changes: 28

October 11 Mello Yello 500
Winner, Mark Martin, Ford
Time of Race: 3:15:47

Cautions: 3 for 12 laps

Average Speed: 153.537 mph

Margin of Victory: 1.88 seconds

Pole Speed: 179.027 mph (Alan Kulwicki, Ford)

Lead Changes: 20

1993

May 30 Coca-Cola 600
Winner, Dale Earnhardt, Chevrolet
Time of Race: 4:07:25
Average Speed: 145.504 mph

Cautions: 7 for 33 laps
Margin of Victory: 3.73
  seconds

Pole Speed: 177.352 mph (Ken
  Schrader, Chevrolet)

Lead Changes: 29

October 10 Mello Yello 500
Winner, Ernie Irvan, Ford
Time of Race: 3:14:31
Average Speed: 154.537 mph

Cautions: 2 for 11 laps
Margin of Victory: 1.83
  seconds

Pole Speed: 177.684 mph (Jeff
  Gordon, Chevrolet)

Lead Changes: 9

1994

May 29 Coca-Cola 600
Winner, Jeff Gordon, Chevrolet
Time of Race: 4:18:10
Average Speed: 139.445 mph

Cautions: 9 for 47 laps
Margin of Victory: 3.91
  seconds

Pole Speed: 181.439 mph (Jeff
  Gordon, Chevrolet)

Lead Changes: 24

October 9 Mello Yello 500
Winner, Dale Jarrett, Chevrolet
Time of Race: 3:26:00
Average Speed: 145.922 mph

Cautions: 7 for 34 laps
Margin of Victory: Under
  caution

Pole Speed: 185.759 mph (Ward
  Burton, Chevrolet)

Lead Changes: 30

1995

May 28 Coca-Cola 600
Winner, Bobby Labonte, Chevrolet
Time of Race: 3:56:55
Average Speed: 151.952 mph

Pole Speed: 183.861 mph (Jeff
   Gordon, Chevrolet)

Cautions: 7 for 33 laps
Margin of Victory: 6.28
   seconds
Lead Changes: 32

October 8 UAW-GM Quality 500
Winner, Mark Martin, Ford
Time of Race: 3:26:48
Average Speed: 145.358 mph

Pole Speed: 180.578 mph (Ricky Rudd, Ford)

Cautions: 7 for 35 laps
Margin of Victory: 0.97
   second
Lead Changes: 19

1996

May 26 Coca-Cola 600
Winner, Dale Jarrett, Ford
Time of Race: 4:03:56
Average Speed: 147.581 mph

Pole Speed: 183.773 mph (Jeff
   Gordon, Chevrolet)

Cautions: 6 for 35 laps
Margin of Victory: 11.982
   seconds
Lead Changes: 20

October 6 UAW-GM Quality 500
Winner, Terry Labonte, Chevrolet
Time of Race: 3:30:00
Average Speed: 143.143 mph

Pole Speed: 184.068 mph (Bobby
   Labonte, Chevrolet)

Cautions: 5 for 37 laps
Margin of Victory: 3.84
   seconds
Lead Changes: 21

1997

May 25 Coca-Cola 600
Winner, Jeff Gordon, Chevrolet
Time of Race: 3:39:10
Average Speed: 136.745 mph

Pole Speed: 184.3 mph (Jeff
 Gordon, Chevrolet)

Cautions: 7 for 50 laps
Margin of Victory: 0.468
 second
Lead Changes: 27

October 5 UAW-GM Quality 500
Winner, Dale Jarrett, Ford
Time of Race: 3:28:17
Average Speed: 144.323 mph

Pole Speed: 184.256 mph (Geoffrey
 Bodine, Ford)

Cautions: 4 for 33 laps
Margin of Victory: 4.142
 seconds
Lead Changes: 20

1998

May 24 Coca-Cola 600
Winner, Jeff Gordon, Chevrolet
Time of Race: 4:23:53
Average Speed: 136.424 mph

Pole Speed: 182.976 mph (Jeff
 Gordon, Chevrolet)

Cautions: 8 for 49 laps
Margin of Victory: 0.41
 second
Lead Changes: 33

October 4 UAW-GM Quality 500
Winner, Mark Martin, Ford
Time of Race: 4:04:01
Average Speed: 123.188 mph

Pole Speed: 181.69 mph (Derrike
 Cope, Pontiac)

Cautions: 11 for 65 laps
Margin of Victory: 1.11
 seconds
Lead Changes: 17

1999

May 30 Coca-Cola 600
Winner, Jeff Burton, Ford
Time of Race: 3:57:50
Average Speed: 151.367 mph

Cautions: 5 for 23 laps
Margin of Victory: 0.574
second

Pole Speed: 185.23 mph (Bobby
Labonte, Pontiac)

Lead Changes: 23

October 11 UAW-GM Quality 500
Winner, Jeff Gordon, Chevrolet
Time of Race: 3:07:31
Average Speed: 160.306 mph

Cautions: 2 for 9 laps
Margin of Victory: 0.851
second

Pole Speed: 185.682 mph (Bobby
Labonte, Pontiac)

Lead Changes: 21

2000

May 28 Coca-Cola 600
Winner, Matt Kenseth, Ford
Time of Race: 4:12:23
Average Speed: 142.64 mph

Cautions: 7 for 38 laps
Margin of Victory: 0.573
second

Pole Speed: 186.034 mph (Dale
Earnhardt Jr., Chevrolet)

Lead Changes: 25

October 8 UAW-GM Quality 500
Winner, Bobby Labonte, Pontiac
Time of Race: 3:44:57
Average Speed: 133.63 mph

Cautions: 9 for 51 laps
Margin of Victory: 1.166
seconds

Pole Speed: 185.561 mph (Fireball
Roberts, Pontiac)

Lead Changes: 46

2001

May 27 Coca-Cola 600
Winner, Jeff Burton, Ford
Time of Race: 4:20:40
Average Speed: 138.107 mph

Cautions: 6 for 45 laps
Margin of Victory: 3.190 seconds

Pole Speed: 185.217 mph (Ryan Newman, Ford)
Lead Changes: 28

October 7 UAW-GM Quality 500
Winner, Sterling Marlin, Dodge
Time of Race: 3:36:15
Average Speed: 139.006 mph

Cautions: 8 for 40 laps
Margin of Victory: 6.002 seconds

Pole Speed: 185.147 mph (Jimmy Spencer, Ford)
Lead Changes: 19

2002

May 26 Coca-Cola Racing Family 600
Winner, Mark Martin, Ford
Time of Race: 4:21:23
Average Speed: 137.729 mph

Cautions: 9 for 48 laps
Margin of Victory: 0.468 second

Pole Speed: 186.464 mph (Jimmie Johnson, Chevrolet)
Lead Changes: 21

October 13 UAW-GM Quality 500
Winner, Jamie McMurray, Dodge
Time of Race: 3:32:28
Average Speed: 141.481 mph

Cautions: 5 for 33 laps
Margin of Victory: 0.350 second

Pole Speed: No Time Trials
Lead Changes: 23

2003

May 25 Coca-Cola 600
Winner, Jimmie Johnson, Chevrolet
Time of Race: 3:16:50

Cautions: 8 for 46 laps

Average Speed: 126.198 mph

Pole Speed: 185.312 mph (Ryan
Newman, Dodge)

Margin of Victory: Under
caution
Lead Changes: 16

October 11 UAW-GM Quality 500
Winner, Tony Stewart, Chevrolet
Time of Race: 3:30:24
Average Speed: 142.871 mph

Pole Speed: 186.657 mph (Ryan
Newman, Dodge)

Cautions: 5 for 31 laps
Margin of Victory: 0.608
- second
Lead Changes: 15

2004

May 30 Coca-Cola 600
Winner, Jimmie Johnson, Chevrolet
Time of Race: 4:12:10
Average Speed: 142.763 mph

Pole Speed: 187.052 mph (Jimmie
Johnson, Chevrolet)

Cautions: 7 for 37 laps
Margin of Victory: Under
caution
Lead Changes: 16

October 16 UAW-GM Quality 500
Winner, Jimmie Johnson, Chevrolet
Time of Race: 3:50:51
Average Speed: 130.214 mph

Pole Speed: 188.877 mph (Ryan
Newman, Dodge)

Cautions: 11 for 53 laps
Margin of Victory: 1.727
seconds
Lead Changes: 18

2005

May 29 Coca-Cola 600
Winner, Jimmie Johnson, Chevrolet
Time of Race: 5:13:52
Average Speed: 114.698 mph

Pole Speed: 192.988 mph (Ryan
Newman, Dodge)

Cautions: 22 for 103 laps
Margin of Victory: 0.027
second
Lead Changes: 37

October 15 UAW-GM Quality 500
Winner, Jimmie Johnson, Chevrolet
Time of Race: 4:11:18
Average Speed: 120.334 mph

Cautions: 15 for 84 laps
Margin of Victory: 0.309 second

Pole Speed: 193.216 mph (Elliott Sadler, Ford)

Lead Changes: 35

2006

May 28 Coca-Cola 600
Winner, Kasey Kahne, Dodge
Time of Race: 4:39:25
Average Speed: 128.84 mph

Cautions: 15 for 66 laps
Margin of Victory: 2.114 seconds

Pole Speed: 187.865 mph (Fireball Roberts, Pontiac)

Lead Changes: 37

October 14 Bank of America 500
Winner, Kasey Kahne, Dodge
Time of Race: 3:47:29
Average Speed: 132.142 mph

Cautions: 10 for 52 laps
Margin of Victory: 1.624 seconds

Pole Speed: 191.469 mph (Scott Riggs, Dodge)

Lead Changes: 34

2007

May 27 Coca-Cola 600
Winner, Casey Mears, Chevrolet
Time of Race: 4:36:27
Average Speed: 130.222 mph

Cautions: 13 for 62 laps
Margin of Victory: 9.561 seconds

Pole Speed: 185.312 mph (Ryan Newman, Dodge)

Lead Changes: 29

October 13 Bank of America 500
Winner, Jeff Gordon, Chevrolet

Time of Race: 4:00:58

Average Speed: 125.868 mph

Pole Speed: 189.394 mph (Ryan Newman, Dodge)

Cautions: 15 for 62 laps

Margin of Victory: 0.579 second

Lead Changes: 26

2008

May 25 Coca-Cola 600
Winner, Kasey Kahne, Dodge
Time of Race: 4:25:09

Average Speed: 135.772 mph

Pole Speed: 185.433 mph (Kyle Busch, Toyota)

Cautions: 11 for 50 laps

Margin of Victory: 10.203 seconds

Lead Changes: 37

October 1 Bank of America 500
Winner, Jeff Burton, Chevrolet
Time of Race: 3:44:50

Average Speed: 133.699 mph

Pole Speed: No Time Trials

Cautions: 10 for 49 laps

Margin of Victory: 0.946 second

Lead Changes: 24

2009

May 25 Coca-Cola 600
Winner, David Reutimann, Toyota
Time of Race: 2:48:59

Average Speed: 120.899 mph

Pole Speed: 188.475 mph (Ryan Newman, Chevrolet)

Cautions: 6 for 40 laps

Margin of Victory: Under caution

Lead Changes: 14

October 17 NASCAR Banking 500 Only From Bank of America
Winner, Jimmie Johnson, Chevrolet
Time of Race: 3:38:22

Average Speed: 137.658 mph

Cautions: 10 for 42 laps

Margin of Victory: 2.303 seconds

Pole Speed: 192.376 mph (Jimmie
Johnson, Chevrolet)

Lead Changes: 22

2010

May 30 Coca-Cola 600
Winner, Kurt Busch, Dodge
Time of Race: 4:08:20
Average Speed: 144.966 mph

Cautions: 8 for 34 laps
Margin of Victory: 0.737
second

Pole Speed: 187.546 mph (Ryan
Newman, Chevrolet)

Lead Changes: 33

October 16 Bank of America 500
Winner, Jamie McMurray, Chevrolet
Time of Race: 3:34:07
Average Speed: 140.391 mph

Cautions: 9 for 39 laps
Margin of Victory: 1.866
seconds

Pole Speed: 191.544 mph (Jeff
Gordon, Chevrolet)

Lead Changes: 27

2011

May 29 Coca-Cola 600
Winner, Kevin Harvick, Chevrolet
Time of Race: 4:33:14
Average Speed: 132.414 mph

Cautions: 14 for 64 laps
Margin of Victory: 0.703
second

Pole Speed: 192.089 mph (Fireball
Roberts, Pontiac)

Lead Changes: 38

October 15 Bank of America 500
Winner, Matt Kenseth, Ford
Time of Race: 3:25:37
Average Speed: 146.194 mph

Cautions: 8 for 34 laps
Margin of Victory: 0.968
second

Pole Speed: 191.959 mph (Tony
Stewart, Chevrolet)

Lead Changes: 16

2012

May 27 Coca-Cola 600
Winner, Kasey Kahne, Chevrolet
Time of Race: 3:51:14
Average Speed: 155.687 mph

Cautions: 5 for 23 laps
Margin of Victory: 4.295 seconds

Pole Speed: 192.94 mph (Fireball Roberts, Pontiac)

Lead Changes: 31

October 13 Bank of America 500
Winner, Clint Bowyer, Toyota
Time of Race: 3:14:01
Average Speed: 154.935 mph

Cautions: 5 for 23 laps
Margin of Victory: 0.417 second

Pole Speed: 193.708 mph (Greg Biffle, Ford)

Lead Changes: 20

NASCAR SPRINT ALL-STAR RACE

1985—Darrell Waltrip
1986—Bill Elliott
1987—Dale Earnhardt
1988—Terry Labonte
1989—Rusty Wallace
1990—Dale Earnhardt
1991—Davey Allison
1992—Davey Allison
1993—Dale Earnhardt
1994—Geoffrey Bodine
1995—Jeff Gordon
1996—Michael Waltrip
1997—Jeff Gordon
1998—Mark Martin
1999—Terry Labonte
2000—Dale Earnhardt Jr.

2001—Jeff Gordon
2002—Ryan Newman
2003—Jimmie Johnson
2004—Matt Kenseth
2005—Mark Martin
2006—Jimmie Johnson
2007—Kevin Harvick
2008—Kasey Kahne
2009—Tony Stewart
2010—Kurt Busch
2011—Carl Edwards
2012—Jimmie Johnson

BIBLIOGRAPHY

Fielden, Greg. *Forty Years of Stock Car Racing: The Beginning 1949–1958.* Galfield Press, 1987.

———. *Forty Years of Stock Car Racing: Big Bucks and Boycotts 1965–1971.* Galfield Press, 1989.

———. *Forty Years of Stock Car Racing: The Modern Era 1972–1989.* Galfield Press, 1990.

———. *Forty Years of Stock Car Racing: The Superspeedway Boom 1959–1964.* Galfield Press, 1988.

Granger, Gene. "Tim Flock." *American Racing Classics.* Griggs Publishing Company, Inc., January 1993.

Hickman, Herman. "Curtis Turner." *American Racing Classics.* Griggs Publishing Company, Inc., April 1992.

Hunter, Jim, and David Pearson. *21 Forever: The Story of Stock Car Driver David Pearson.* Strode Publishers Inc., 1980.

Kelly, Bob. *NASCAR Winston Cup 1994.* UMI Publications Inc., 1994.

———. *NASCAR Winston Cup 2001.* UMI Publications Inc. and NASCAR, 2001.

Neely, Bill. *Grand National: The Autobiography of Richard Petty as Told to Bill Neely.* Henry Regnery Company, 1971.

Newspapers and Periodicals

2012 Charlotte Motor Speedway Coca-Cola 600 program.

Charlotte Motor Speedway. Press release for 2011 Bank of America 500.

International Motorsports Hall of Fame 1992 induction program.

McCredie, Gary. "Waltrip Outruns Gant for Big $$ Victory." *Grand National Scene*, May 30, 1985.

——. "Was It a 'Really Big Show?' You Bet It Was." *Grand National Scene*, May 21, 1987.

Muhleman, Max. "Charlotte's Bold Venture Into Racing 35 Years Ago." 1960 World 600 program.

NASCAR Winston Cup Scene (1994, 2000, 2001).

New York Times (May 1995).

Smith, Bruton. Interview. By Deb Williams. *NASCAR Winston Cup Scene* (1997).

Stinson, Tom. "No. 2—And Counting." *NASCAR Winston Cup Scene*, May 22, 1997.

Thomas, Theresa. "First North Carolina Governor Once Owned Charlotte Motor Speedway Site." 1960 World 600 program.

Waid, Steve. "Earnhardt Guns 'Em Down for Victory No. 3." *Winston Cup Scene*, May 27, 1993.

——. "Earnhardt Wins Amid Controversial Finish." *Grand National Scene*, May 21, 1987.

White, Rea. "Sterling Performance." *NASCAR Winston Cup Scene*, October 17, 2002.

INTERNET REFERENCE SITES

Britannica Encyclopedia, www.britannica.com.

CBS News, www.cbsnews.com.

Charlotte Motor Speedway, www.charlottemotorspeedway.com.

Charlotte Observer, www.charlotteobserver.com.

Charlotte Observer, www.ThatsRacin.com.

CNN/SI, Cnnsi.com.

Curtis Turner Museum, www.curtisturnermuseum.com.

Hickory Metro Sports Commission, www.hickorymetrosportscommission.com.

McCormick, Steve, About.com Guide.

Projects of Interest, www.projectsofinterest.com.

Racing-Reference.info, www.racing-reference.info.

Reference for Business, www.referenceforbusiness.com.

Speedway Children's Charities, www.speedwaycharities.org.

Speedway Motorsports Inc., www.speedwaymotorsports.com.

Sports Illustrated/CNN, www.sportsillustrated.cnn.com.

Wikipedia, www.wikipedia.org.

INDEX

ABOUT THE AUTHOR

Deb Williams is an award-winning motorsports journalist who has covered NASCAR for thirty years. She began covering weekly races at New Asheville (North Carolina) Speedway while a student at East Tennessee State University and continued after becoming the sports editor at the newspaper in Waynesville, North Carolina. Upon joining United Press International in Raleigh, she began covering NASCAR's top two series. After leaving UPI, she spent eighteen years with the publication *NASCAR Winston Cup Scene*, serving as its editor for ten years. Her numerous honors include being the first woman to receive the Henry T. McLemore Award for continued outstanding motorsports journalism, the first person to receive the Russ Catlin Award two consecutive years and a two-time recipient of the National Motorsports Press Association Writer of the Year award. Since leaving *Scene*, her work has appeared on RacinToday.com and in many publications, including *Chicken Soup for the Soul: NASCAR*. Her other books include *The Evolution of NASCAR: A Historical Collection*, *Ryan Newman: Engineering Speed* and *Ray Evernham: Racer, Innovator, Leader*.

A Canton, North Carolina native, she has taught the Evolution of Southern Motorsports at Appalachian State University and has been interviewed for historical motorsports shows that have aired on ESPN and SPEED (now Fox Sports 1).

Visit us at
www.historypress.net

....

This title is also available as an e-book